Croyde, North Devon

9-12 September 2005

Amanda Derrick's

"Big" Birthday Celebration

@ South West Surf Club

"Unless you've tried it - its hard to believe it can be so exciting + addictive" - the Surf South West brochure. Couldn't agree more - thanks for the invite - I am now hooked and Happy 50 birthday! Love Philippa XX

Fabulous as so! Thanks for inviting me to your wonderful celebration! I hope you enjoyed it as much as the rest of us xx

Amanda, what a 'totally awesome' way to celebrate your birthday. Hope your memories will remain as vivid as mine. Don't let go of the rails too early! Love J x

Marvela zinoox Ever ambitious! What a great weekend - it all rolls! went so well. Had enough food to look like the lady on Page 181. I wanted to look like but alas it was not to be! Thank you for a great experience - it was fantastic + great fun.
Love Annie x

Page 156, that's us! Brilliant fun, a new experience I'd never have tried without you. I dread to think what you will have us doing Amanda - for your 60th! Love Judith xx

Typically You! A dynamic + different, fantastic weekend to celebrate your birthday. What a wonderful time! Love Helen XX

Amanda! You are inspirational! Without you I would not have cycled 50 miles or braved a surf board! Thanks to being 50!! Love Bekki x

Fantastic birthday celebration, very pleased to be part of it even if I didn't get beyond my knees! Great team spirit and lots of fun. Love Paula

Amanda - hope you've had as wonderful a weekend as I have! You're a star! Love, Aileen

You never thought I'd do it! I never thought I'd do it!! But I did!!! Great birthday celebration... and I really enjoyed my surfing experience to. Happy Birthday. Love Gill

Dear Amanda. There's no one else who shows me the best of Britain like you do. To think I'd moved 3500 miles to surf!! Thank you for inviting me to your 50th celebration! It & you are inspirational, exciting & so creative. And the best of friends!! All hugs - Margaret.

I hope you enjoyed your surfing - I'm sorry I'm such a wuss - but I've had a lovely time anyway! Ros x

Blue Heaven

The cold threatening waves of Victoria...
an isolated beach on the edge of the wild.

Blue **Heaven**

The Story of Australian Surfing

Murray Walding

Hardie Grant Books

Published in 2003
by Hardie Grant Books
12 Claremont Street
South Yarra, Victoria 3141, Australia
www.hardiegrant.com.au

National Library of Australia Cataloguing-in-Publication Data:
Walding, Murray.
        Blue heaven.

        Bibliography.
        Includes index.
        ISBN 1 74066 008 0.

        1. Surfing - Australia. 2. Surfing - Australia - History.
        I. Title.

        797.320994

Edited by Sally Moss
Cover and text design and layout by Phil Campbell
Printed and bound in Singapore by Imago Productions Pte. Ltd

10 9 8 7 6 5 4 3 2 1

Acknowledgements

Surfing developed as a pastime, rather than a sport and as a consequence, much of its history has, apart from contest results, gone unrecorded. The history laid down in this book has come from the memories of the colorful characters in surfing's past.

I'd like to thank the following people who were extremely helpful by either recounting their stories and recollections, or by allowing me access to their archives. Joe Sweeney, Shane Clarke, Hayden Burford, Ken Pollard, Scott Dillon, Dave O'Donnell, Reggae Ellis, Bruce Usher, Jack Eden, Dave Storey, Terry Edwards, Barry Bennett, Gail Couper, John Witzig, Dick Evans, Alby Falzon, John Pennings, Doug Warbrick, Mick Mock, Bruce Usher, George Greenough, Paul Witzig, Rod Brooks, Al Hunt, Ted Bainbridge, Randy Rarick, Alan Atkins, Ross Renwick, Nick Carroll, Darryl Homan, Peter Clifton, Rennie Ellis, Loz Smith, Kevin Merryfield, Brian Cole, Fred Lang, Tony Edwards, Jeff Raglus, Paul Harris, Graham Wall, Gary Birdsall, Roy Bisson, Midget Farrelly, Wayne Lynch, Dennis Callinan, Wayne Bartholomew, Paul Hough, Doug Rogers, Frank McWilliams, Wayne Golding, Dare Jennings and Greg Noll.

When memories fade, photographs remain, so I also thank the photographers whose works grace the pages of this book. Without these beautiful images, any history of surfing would be incomplete. My thanks to Dick Hoole, Simon Williams, Jeff Carter, Martin Tullemans, David Milnes, Bob Weekes, Scott Wintle, Joli, Steve Ryan, Bruce Channon, Trevor Lemke, Monty Weber.

Thanks to the various archives who allowed me access to their material: State Library of Victoria, State Library of New South Wales, Museum Victoria, National Archives of Australia, Picture Australia, The Geelong Advertiser, and the National Library of Australia, Surfing Australia, The Surfrider Foundation, and Surfworld Surfing Museum.

My thanks go to the staff at Hardie Grant, in particular, Tracy O'Shaughnessy and also to design guru Phil Campbell.

Thank you to Bob Smith for checking the facts and correcting my omissions; Peter Troy and Albie Thoms for their wealth of invaluable knowledge; and David Sumpter for his continuing support, advice and enthusiasm.

On a personal note, thanks have to go to Jughead, Moon, Quinny, Gomer, Nuge, Dick, JR, Dave, Laubs, Tibbs and all the other guys on the east coast who I grew up surfing with.

I also must thank my parents who let me go surfing, and turned a blind eye to what that really meant! And my sister who, strangely enough, first took me surfing with her greasy hodad boyfriends! And my brother, who gave me my first board and taught me just enough and let me discover the rest myself.

Thanks to my great family and closest friends – Sharon, Daniel and Dallas.

⊡ A warm early morning tube on the Gold Coast, before the crowd swarms into the line-up.

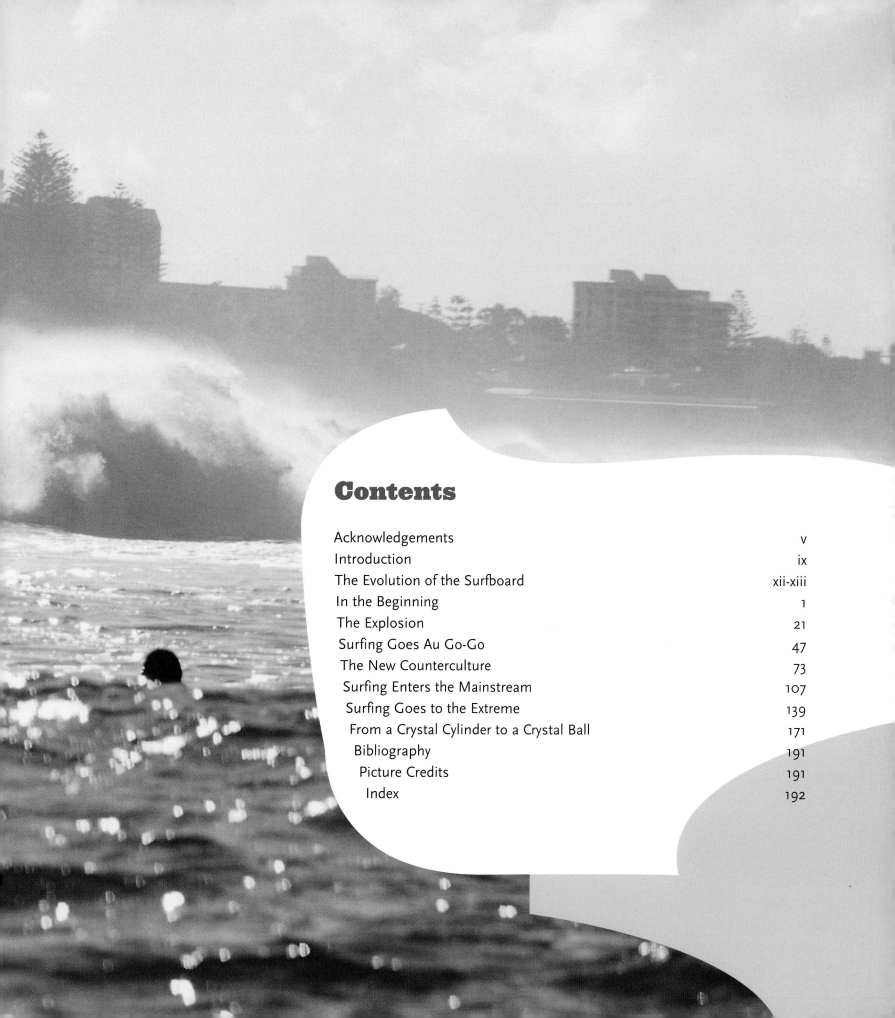

Contents

Introduction

I grew up on the beach. I could see the water from my bedroom window, and the beach was where I spent my summers … along with everyone else! Each summer, holiday makers swarmed from the local railway station and clogged our beach with suntan oil, fringed towels, Donald Duck X29 wrappers and icy-pole sticks.

There was a whole bunch of us: me and my gawky teenage mates in Ockanui shorts, the slender local girls in terry-towelling bikinis, all of us hanging out on the beach wall in front of the lifesaving club, checking out the sweaty summer's mayhem.

In other words, our summers were just like everyone else's.

But there was one thing our beach lacked: surf!

My childhood was spent on flat, lazy Port Phillip Bay. How we envied the young kids who perched on their local beach walls in Sydney, Queensland or Perth. We knew those kids had surf – the surf magazines had told us.

We did have waves of a sort. But they were slop – the kind of windblown junk that surges across Port Phillip in a big southerly blow. Never a clean, ruler-edged groundswell, never an offshore breeze. But there's surf in Victoria alright, great surf. It was just that we couldn't get at it. The closest real surf spots were on the Mornington Peninsula where there was a strip of coast full of classy reef breaks and thunderous, isolated ocean beaches; it was there that I rode my first *real* surf.

Now, to many people the quintessential *real* Aussie surf experience is found on an isolated beach, on the edge of the wild, where the wilderness experience makes up for less-than-perfect waves. For others, perfect surf is perfect surf, no matter how many high-rise towers disfigure the horizon.

But really, is there anything better than a hot summer's morning at your own beach, when the crowd is just starting to fill the car park and the clubbies have put up the flags, and to the edge of the flagged area there is a nice tight right-hander breaking waist-high over the sandbar? From the water you can faintly hear the clubhouse PA picking up the radio – maybe it's The Beatles you can hear, or is it Moby, or both?

Sure, the water's starting to get crowded, but the next wave of the set is peaking just in front of you.

And it's all yours.

⬅ Summer holidays... the beach wall in front of the lifesaving club, checking out the sweaty summer's mayhem.

➡ For some, perfect surf is perfect surf, no matter how many high rise towers disfigure the horizon.

The Evolution of the Surfboard

c. 1905 Tommy Tanna, a Solomon Islander, introduces surf shooting at Manly beach. It will later be called body surfing.

c. 1912 The first solid timber surfboards arrive on our shores, brought to Australia by tourists returning from Hawaii, but few Australians can master them.

December 1914 Duke Kahanamoku demonstrates surfboard riding on Sydney beaches. Isabel Letham accompanies him in tandem rides.

c. 1920 Small timber boards, similar to Hawaiian paipos but longer, appear on coastal beaches throughout the country but are too thin to stand on.

1934 Frank Adler builds the first hollow surfboard. Dr 'Saxon' Crackenthorp develops the Australian surf ski. Dr Smithers introduces the inflatable Surf-o-Plane.

c. 1935 Californian surfers attach skegs to their boards.

1937 The Surf Lifesaving Association officially adopts the surf ski for rescue work.

1946 California's Pete Peterson and Brant Goldworthy pioneer the first fibreglass-coated surfboard. Another Californian, Bob Simmons, continues his experiments with fin design, nose lift and rail shapes. His designs revolutionise surfboard design.

c. 1952 The first balsa boards appear in the Australian surf, but their advantages are largely ignored.

November 1956 Australian surfers witness Californian lifeguards hot-dogging on fibreglass/balsa Malibu boards at Torquay. Within seven days, Bill Clymer produces a hollow ply copy.

c. 1958 The first commercial shipments of balsa arrive in the country and are quickly snaffled by Sydney board builders who struggle to keep up with the demand. Roger Keiran builds Australia's first fibreglass-and-balsa Malibu board.

c. 1960 Greg McDonagh 'blows' his first styrofoam blank.

c. 1963 Thousands of polystyrene blanks are blown as the surfing craze explodes.

1965 George Greenough unveils his fibreglass spoon at Point Cartwright in Queensland.

1966 Midget Farrelly cuts down the weight on his boards by using stringerless blanks. George Greenough fine-tunes the fin on Sam, Nat Young's thin, responsive 9'4" stick. On Sam, Nat wins the 66 world title.

1967 The deep-vee, twang-finned Stubbie makes its debut and sounds the death knell for traditional longboards.

February 1968 The Pintail arrives, a combination of ideas from guru shaper Dick Brewer in Hawaii and Farrelly at home. It sounds the death knell for the Stubbie.

Mid-1968 The Pintail shortens and evolves into the Tracker and Pocket Rocket.

Early 1969 Wayne Lynch's International Involvement model, a double-ended roundpin, made by Adelaide's John Arnold, hits the shops. Ted Spencer's White Kite model is released by Shane Surfboards.

May 1970 Boards shrink to less than 6 feet in length. Californian Rolf Aurness wins the 1970 World Titles on a seven-foot-something rounded Pintail.

1970–71 The Shane pop-out boards capture a huge slice of the Sydney market. Side Slippers, a dead-end street in surfing's evolution, appear then rapidly disappear.

Tom Hoye, another Californian shaper, arrives in Sydney with templates for the first-generation twin fins.

Wayne Lynch and Nat Young flirt with keel fins made by Torquay's Pat Morgan, but they prove to be another dead-end street.

Michael Peterson wails at Kirra Point on a short single fin that looks like its template has been traced from his mum's ironing board.

1973 Down-rail, rounded Pintails become the most common board in the water. Small bumps in the rail line (fliers) prove popular.

1974 In California, Tom Morey markets his flexible Boogie board. The DIY kit is available by mail order only.

1975 Mark Richards takes up the Hawaiian-designed Stinger.

May 1976 Hawaiian Reno Abellira rides an ugly short twin fin in the 1976 Coke Classic. Mark Richards shows some interest, then popularises the second-generation twin fins.

1980 Frank Williams, a Sydney shaper experiments with a three-finned surfboard. Simon Anderson shows a little interest.

Grant Kenny wins the first Australian surf ski ('goat boat') title.

Some surfers drag out old Malibu boards for a bit of fun.

April 1981 Simon Anderson wins the Rip Curl Pro at Bells Beach on a three-fin board he calls a Thruster.

c. 1983 Geoff McCoy designs a reverse tear-drop short-board called a Lazer-Zap.

1984 Cheyne Horan rides a Lazer-Zap fitted with a Lexcen-inspired star fin to victory in the Rip Curl Pro.

c. 1985 Tom Curren popularises the squash-tail Thruster on his way to winning the world title.

Knackers Kernovske wins the first official Australian longboard title.

c. 1992 Thrusters become thinner and develop flipped-up noses and increased rocker.

c.1995 Brian Whitty develops the interchangeable fin system, the FCS.

Late 1990s More and more surfers take to the water on mid-length boards, enjoying the increased flotation. Small changes to the Thruster design are heralded as 'design breakthroughs'.

A sunny day at a Sydney beach in the early 1900s; just perfect for surf bathing.

In The **Beginning**

Yes, in summer it can be hard to find a spot in the sand big enough to spread a beach towel, let alone to wax up your board. Crowds of sun seekers are everywhere – surfing, sunbaking or just plain posing. In winter, there's more room to stretch out. Even in the bleakest winter conditions, Australians still feel the need to wander the beach, picking up silvered arms of driftwood, peering into rock pools. Surfing and the beach. Both have become defining elements of our culture, as identifiable as *Neighbours*, as pervasive as infotainment.

It's hard to imagine a time when this wasn't so. And yet, strange as it may seem, there was a time when surfing and swimming (bathing as it was then called) were discouraged at Australian beaches.

Although not banned outright, bathing in the surf during daylight hours (designated as being 7 a.m. to 6 p.m. in the late 1800s on Sydney's northern beaches) was prohibited for seven decades from 1833. These strict regulations were introduced to enforce standards of dress along the colony's beaches. Local aldermen were concerned that bathers of both sexes were bathing and changing in view of 'the general public' and large fines were imposed for those caught in a state of dress that did not cover the body from the neck to the knee.

Despite the regulations, crowds still took to the water at every opportunity and nude swimming at secluded beaches was common even in the early 1900s. But if you chose to swim in public, even during restricted hours, you needed a clingy, misshapen, woollen, neck to knee swimsuit – and a place to change. Accordingly, many councils erected sea baths. These rickety structures – part pier, part pool – offered some protection from public gaze, currents, undertows and sharks. But they were at the mercy of large surf, and most were repeatedly damaged by winter storms.

At around the same time, small wagons also appeared on the sand. Known as bathing machines, they were introduced from England via South Africa. Our local

versions featured flimsy detachable fencing, much like a baby's play-pen. Hauled into the surf by horses, they provided a very private and very cramped bathing experience and rapidly fell from favour.

Of course, some town fathers were keen to dissuade their constituents from bathing so as to prevent them from drowning, and although rudimentary surf lifesaving societies were in place on Sydney beaches from the mid-1890s, most beaches were not patrolled and few people could swim. Drownings were common at harbour and bayside beaches around the country but on ocean beaches their rate of occurrence was downright alarming.

That scantily clad swimmers continued to throw themselves into the waves at any opportunity – not just to brave the wild surf but, it seemed, to flirt with the ever-present threat of shark attack, must have preyed on the minds of public-minded burghers around the land. And this at a time when it was thought that daylight hours should be reserved for those in meaningful employment, not scoundrels who chose to indulge themselves shamelessly by bathing in the surf instead of working.

Despite the attempts of local councils to dissuade folk from entering the water in indecent clothing, the laws were seldom enforced – for the simple reason that enforcement was fraught with difficulties. Uniformed police stood out like sore thumbs on local beaches and were loath to invoke the by-laws. Often the offenders scarpered before the local constabulary could make any arrests.

⊕ The bathing machine was briefly considered to be a safe option in the surf, but was completely impractical for Australian conditions.

Drownings were common at harbour and bayside beaches around the country but on ocean beaches their rate of occurrence was downright alarming.

'All persons above the age of eight, male or female, shall be so clothed as to prevent exposure or indecency ...'

⊡ Those who felt modest brought their own tent to change in.

⊡ Four young girls having fun on the beach at Lorne, Victoria. Not everyone was took the trouble to be decently dressed. Nude swimming was common – and frowned upon.

⊡ Duke Kahanamoku and his hand-made, finless, sugar-pine surfboard in front of the Freshwater Beach Life Saving Clubhouse in 1914.

Concerns over improper bathing attire were not confined to Sydney beaches. At the Victorian beachside resort of Lorne, bathers wearing indecent clothing so distressed swimmers that the local shire was asked to station police on the beach.

Eventually public pressure on Sydney councils increased as bathers on both sides of the harbour continued to defy the bans. In 1902, Randwick Borough Council passed a by-law permitting all-day bathing, provided that 'all persons above the age of eight, male or female, shall be so clothed as to prevent exposure or indecency'. Waverley Council soon followed suit, but bathers on the city's north side were still not permitted to enter the water after 8 a.m.

The most celebrated of these bathers was William Gocher, editor of the local newspaper the *Manly and North-Sydney News*. Gocher is popularly but incorrectly regarded as having been the first person to openly challenge the bans on surf bathing at Manly when he conducted a brief and inconsequential campaign to have the laws repealed. Over the first weeks of the surf season of October 1902 he used his newspaper to claim not only that the laws were restrictive but that he would openly defy them by bathing at Manly in the middle of the day on each Sunday of the month. After splashing around in knee-deep water for three consecutive weekends without raising any sort of reaction he made his way back to the beach, headed for the local police station and gave himself up. The local magistrate informed him that as he was properly dressed he had committed no offence – and he was never charged.

↑ Ladies taking a lifesaving examination at North Wollongong Beach in 1914. It's unclear just what was being examined!

↑ Sydney socialites at Palm Beach in 1915, with the latest fashions and the latest in surf craft – the solid timber surfboard.

Contemporary accounts gave scant coverage to Gocher's 'campaign' and it was not until 1907, when Gocher was about to leave the colony, that the matter was raised at all, and it now appears likely that Gocher's role was insignificant.

Regardless of the urban myth surrounding William Gocher's actions, within twelve months, Manly Council dispensed with its by-laws and allowed unrestricted bathing at its beaches. Continued pressure from bathers all along the coast forced other councils to do likewise. Swimmers adopted the new vogue of mixed bathing and Australians took to their newest pass-time with renewed vigour.

North of Manly lies tiny Freshwater Beach. Already a favourite haunt of those who chose to ignore regulations and swim nude, Freshwater was to figure in the advance of Oz surf culture when Hawaiian beach boy and Olympic Champion swimmer Duke Kahanamoku was invited to Sydney to swim at the new Domain Baths. While in Sydney, Duke checked out the local beaches and agreed to perform surfboard riding exhibitions at Dee Why, South Steyne and Freshwater. Duke had arrived *sans* board, and when asked why he hadn't thought to include a board with his luggage, he replied, 'We were told the use of boards was not permitted in Australia.' It appears that Duke had learnt this from an American traveller, Alexander Hume Ford.

Ford had established the Outrigger Canoe and Surfboard Club at Waikiki and visited Australia in 1908. He was keen to sample the local surf but was told that while surfboard riding was not unknown it was prohibited.

Primitive copies of Hawaiian boards had been appearing on beaches in both New South Wales and Victoria in the years before the outbreak of World War I and two years before Duke's visit W.H. Walker had demonstrated his skill in standing on a board at Freshwater. In Queensland, Charlie Faulkner had given surf riding displays at Greenmount Beach in 1914, as had Albert Phipps at Southport in the same year, but it seems that few riders were able to master these boards.

If surf bathing was already considered dangerous, the thought of a loose solid timber surfboard bouncing shoreward must have alarmed councils even more. But with the help of a local lumber merchant, Duke Kahanamoku fashioned from sugar pine a surfboard that would suit his needs. The *Daily Telegraph* described it as '8 feet in length, 3 feet in width, 100 lb in weight and narrowed at one end'.

So, on a summer's morning in 1914, Duke Kahanamoku heaved his new board onto his shoulder, strode across the sand, plunged into the Freshwater surf and stunned the crowd on the beach with a display of hard cornering and trick riding the likes of which the locals had never seen before.

Later on that summer's morning, on the beach at Freshwater, Duke approached a young girl by the name of Isabel Letham and asked whether she would accompany him out through the breakers. Isabel agreed and both of them plunged into the surf and made their way out to the break. Duke quickly snared a wave and with Isabel seated on the front half of his board rode back to the beach. Isabel and Duke took several waves, the young girl standing in front of Duke and later being held in his arms as they raced into the shore break.

⬆ Even at the end of the nineteenth century, Australians loved the beach. This windswept expanse of beach and sand-dune is our internationally famous Bondi Beach.

Continued pressure from bathers all along the coast forced other councils to allow unrestricted bathing. Swimmers adopted the new vogue of mixed bathing and Australians took to their newest pass-time with renewed vigour.

➔ The sand-dunes were eventually smothered by homes, flats and carparks. And still people flocked there – Bondi Beach between the wars.

⊕ Claude West of Manly: one of our first surfing heroes.

Today, modern tandem riders compete on a small contest circuit for cash prizes. They train hard and regularly, practising their gymnastic moves on dry sand before paddling out on their high-performance lightweight boards. But back at Freshwater Beach almost a century ago, sixteen-year-old Isabel, an absolute beginner in every sense of the word, was coaxed into the surf for the first time by an Hawaiian Olympic champion – a man now acknowledged as the father of modern surfing and tandem surfs – on a cumbersome, handmade sugar pine plank.

A handmade surfboard, without a fin! Hers was without doubt a feat of unparalleled skill and daring but it would be decades before Australian women would again figure in the development of Australian surfing.

Before leaving Australia, Duke Kahanamoku handed his handmade plank over to local teenager Claude West, and other surfers were quick to copy its design. Duke's board is now a treasured display in the clubhouse of Freshwater Surf Lifesaving Club. Any further development of surfboard riding would have to wait until the end of the Great War.

In the years after the war, lifesaving clubs at popular surf beaches were at odds with the essentially calm-water-oriented Royal Lifesaving Society. These clubs grouped together in 1922 to form the Surf Lifesaving Association of Australia (SLSA). Many of the association's early members were returned servicemen, who felt at home in its regimented and purely male environment.

The surf lifesaving movement preserved the ideals of diligent training, precise parade ground drill, and co-operation – co-operation in the teams who worked tirelessly with the reel and line, making sure that the belt man could swim, free of line tangles, to a victim caught in a rip; co-operation in piloting their sleek boats through the surf. The movement also gave all Aussie males the chance to patrol the beach and, if the opportunity arose, call on their mates, plunge into the surf and return to the beach a hero with a half-drowned swimmer in tow.

For many young men the appeal was irresistible, and during the 1920s and 30s membership swelled, with clubs formed in Queensland, on what later became known as the Gold and Sunshine Coasts and even as far north as Bundaberg. By the early 1930s, similar clubs were operating on the suburban beaches of Perth.

In Victoria, the isolation of surf beaches (most were over ninety-five kilometres from Melbourne), the bone-numbing cold water and the seasonal nature of the southern climate held back initial attempts to form clubs until after World War II. Melbourne's suburban beaches, mostly flat-water affairs, had been protected by lifesavers from Royal Lifesaving Clubs since early in the century. 'Royal' club members, regardless of gender, all performed the same duties, including patrols, but the growing Surf Lifesaving Association movement did not recognise the 'Royal' qualifications and there were no dual affiliation rights. Some Victorian surf lifesaving clubs, like Anglesea and Warrnambool, were originally Royal clubs, but in 1947 both became fully fledged member clubs of the SLSA. The women associates became members of their newly formed auxiliaries.

Regardless of the lack of club development in Australia's southern States, the image of the bronzed lifesaver was culturally enshrined. But the egalitarian sense of duty that

If surf bathing was already considered dangerous, the thought of a loose solid timber surfboard bouncing shoreward must have alarmed councils even more.

Surfing – a defining element of our culture, no matter what the era.

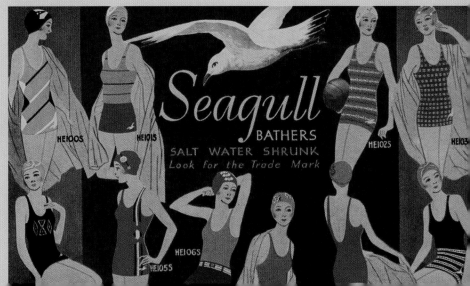

it denoted did not apply to Australian women, who, regardless of their experience in say, Royal Lifesaving Clubs, were not permitted to take the examination for the Surf Bronze Medallion, the SLSA's basic requirement for patrol duties.

On the Gold Coast two clubs boasting lady lifesavers were formed (the Neptunes, and the Dolphins). But most women were encouraged to form a Ladies' Auxiliary attached to an all-male club, their role being to help raise funds for building clubhouses and new equipment.

A women's surf lifesaving club did appear at Yamba, on the New South Wales mid-north coast; and on the Gold Coast two clubs boasting lady lifesavers were formed (the Neptunes, and the Dolphins). But most women were encouraged to form a Ladies' Auxiliary attached to an all-male club, their role being to help raise funds for building clubhouses and new equipment.

Back in the surf, the solid timber boards of Duke's design continued to prove their worth in numerous rescues. By the 1920s, Claude West, who had inherited Duke's board, had become a Manly lifeguard and used his own solid board to rescue three bathers from a group of five who were in difficulties at South Steyne Beach. On another occasion, one of West's rescues turned out to be Australia's Governor-General, but club officials still looked on the surfboard with disdain. Boards were seen as a distraction from the regimented patrols and training drills, and the reel and line remained the favoured method of rescue on Australian surf beaches until the 1970s.

The reel and line apparatus first appeared at Bondi Beach in 1906 and was an immediate success, being responsible for the rescue of two cousins from the surf at Bondi. One of the lads was a young Charlie Smith. Thirty years later, Charlie was a national hero, having by then received not only the accolade of being this country's greatest aviator but also the knighthood that made him Sir Charles Kingsford-Smith.

⊤ Hollow boards were sleek, shiny and finless. They were brutes to control.

◿ Even in the chilly waters of Summerland Beach on Victoria's Phillip Island, people flocked to the water. These thin timber boards were only suitable for lying on and were probably the property of the guesthouse which stood on the headland above the beach.

◸ Five beach belles at Manly, lying on hollow boards. The sixteen-foot toothpick on the far right belongs to Ray Leighton, who took the photo.

The 1920s also saw the rise in popularity of the Australian surfboat. Similar to whaleboats, these clinker-built double enders, later replaced by the smaller and lighter carvel-built boats, were crewed by five tanned and muscly lifesavers. Surfboats became a symbol of bravery, courage and co-operation. Newsreels of Australian beach life were never complete without spectacular footage of these boats climbing up mountains of water or ploughing sideways through the foam.

Their reputation for saving lives became legend when in early 1931, at Sydney's Bronte Beach, the North Steyne boat *Bluebottle*, with Rastus Evans at the sweep oar, rescued twenty-six lifesavers swept into trouble during a carnival. Evans took *Bluebottle*'s crew out through the surf three times to complete the rescue. Rastus and *Bluebottle* had already become famous in the previous year when he and his crew had rowed out to the Queenscliff Bombora. The Bombie – not just a fat, rolling offshore peak but a genuine brute of a wave five hundred metres from shore – must have seemed just the challenge for Evans. It was he who held the safety of *Bluebottle* and his crew in his own hands as surely as he grasped the sweep oar. It would be through his skill in piloting *Bluebottle* that they would crack the Bombie or swim.

They swam.

The Bombie was too strong even for Rastus Evans to master, and he was later forced to give an assurance to the committee men of North Steyne Club that neither he nor the crew would ever again try to crack the Bombie. (The Queenscliff Bombora was finally conquered in 1949, when a Freshwater boat hooked three successive mountains of water and rowed back to the beach to tell the tale.)

Not long after Rastus and *Bluebottle* featured in the mass rescue at Bronte Beach, three new surf craft appeared on Australian beaches, when bodysurfing – or surf shooting, as it was then known – was still the most common form of surfing. The solid timber

Black Sunday The heroism and bravery of Australian surf lifesavers reached legendary status one hot February day at Bondi Beach in 1938 – a day now known by surf lifesavers as Black Sunday.

A steaming hot, late summer's day had attracted tens of thousands of swimmers to Bondi, who cooled off in the tough but small surf. By late afternoon, the dropping tide had enticed a large crowd of swimmers onto a shallow offshore sandbar in the middle of the beach, but suddenly, as the tide started to turn, a larger than average set of waves steamed out of the deep water and broke across the shallow sandbar.

Each wave of the set was larger than its predecessor, and a churning sweep of water washed all those standing on the bar off their feet, tumbling them shoreward and into a deep hole and rip that now churned with choppy spume. As the water surged through the rip and headed back out to sea, it dragged some two hundred swimmers with it.

Bondi beltmen quickly dashed into the water but their efforts were thwarted by drowning swimmers who took hold of the line in their panic, their combined weight pulling the beltmen under. The lines were frantically hauled in, each with a spluttering beltman and dozens of half drowned swimmers. But dozens of swimmers had been swept out behind the waves, out of the reach of reel and line.

Fortunately, the Bondi clubhouse was full of willing hands – many club members had arrived earlier in the afternoon to take place in the club's regular Sunday arvo club race, and seventy lifesavers snatched up anything and everything that would float, struck out into the surf and hauled near-dead swimmers back to the sand.

Those returned to the beach half alive were laid out wherever a flat surface could be found and teams of volunteers performed resuscitation in relays. Although it initially seemed that around fifty swimmers would not be revived, the final tally of deaths was five, all men.

No awards for bravery were ever made on that day as no individuals could be singled out, but the brave Bondi clubmembers who rescued so many are still remembered for their selfless heroism and feats of bravery that have few equals in Australian history.

The blunt-sterned, carvel-built surfboat eventually replaced the double ender and quickly became the most effective craft for surf rescue work.

PLEASURE, aye! and THRIFT! with ADVANX PRODUCTS

The primary aim when riding a surfo was to see how many swimmers you could run over, enjoying each soft bounce as you mowed down the glistening bodies diving for cover in the shore break.

⬆⬈ Surf-O-Planes and Vita-Tan tents on the beach at Kirra on Queensland's Gold Coast. Vita-Tan was replaced by zinc cream and later by 15+ sunblock. The Surf-O-Plane was common in our surf until the 1960s. Its current equivalent is the body board.

boards of World War I vintage had grown in length and, although sleeker and stiffened with hardwood and pine stringers, were still a nightmare to handle. It was hard enough to lug them down to the surf's edge, much less control them as they hurtled shoreward. What was needed was a method of constructing a durable board that lacked the excessive weight.

The breakthrough came from the United States where Tom Blake, an experienced and somewhat offbeat water man, inspired by Duke Kahanamoku and early Hawaiian boards on display in Honolulu's Bishop Museum, developed a board made from redwood and a new high-tech material: plywood. The board was hollow and lightweight – manoeuvrable but still durable. It quickly became the preferred equipment for lifeguards throughout California and eventually the design made its way to our shores. The first Australian version, built by Maroubra board rider Frank Adler, appeared in 1934. These hollow boards quickly became popular at our beaches and for a time lifesaving carnivals featured surfboard races.

Almost simultaneously, another surf craft debuted in the Sydney waves. It too was hollow, but it was wider than the normal hollow boards. It also featured a long tapered tail, nose lift and straps for the rider's feet. It was the Australian surf ski. Developed by Dr 'Saxon' Crackenthorp of Manly, these boards were originally around three metres in length, but the design was quickly transformed and they became shiny sixteen-foot (five-metre) needles. They were nicknamed 'toothpicks' and in sizeable surf they were not any easier to ride.

The SLSA officially adopted surf skis as rescue boards in 1937. Later (and longer) versions were also designed to take two riders. The single versions could be ridden – with considerable skill – standing up, but they were more often ridden sitting down, the rider using a paddle for steering. Whether ridden seated or standing, they could be lethal. Their length and hard square rails made cornering almost impossible and once they began to tilt and bounce sideways the finless tail would slide out, leaving the rider heading sideways to the beach with five metres of varnished ply bucking out of control in the whitewater. They could take out handfuls of swimmers in the one go before they reached dry sand. Such scenes of carnage in the surf continued until the end of the 1950s and toothpicks were still common in the surf in the 70s.

Snowy McAlister, a champion surfer from the 1920s, when he won three Australian titles on his solid board, took to the hollow boards and was a common sight at Manly's Fairy Bower. Snowy was a real stalwart of the SLSA and board-riding organisations and he continued surfing his toothpick at the Bower until the mid-1970s.

Much more fun, and safer too, was another new surf craft, the Surf-o-Plane. Also appearing in 1934, this inflatable rubber mat was the invention of yet another doctor, a Dr Smithers of Bronte. Soon every beach had entrepreneurs hiring out these exciting rubber mats, often seen stacked in piles beside a small stand

⬆ Three real beauties, and the finalists of the 1952 Miss Pacific Quest at Manly.

The SLSA officially adopted surf skis as rescue boards in 1937 … They could take out handfuls of swimmers in the one go before they reached dry sand.

manned by a sun-blackened gent who kept a close check on how long each 'surfo' had been in the water.

The primary aim when riding a surfo was to see how many swimmers you could run over, enjoying each soft bounce as you mowed down the glistening bodies diving for cover in the shore break. When the surfo was inflated just right you could pull the handles down and back and it would fold in half then nose dive, and the skilled rider would somersault underwater. And pop up again at the back of the wave, nasal passages flushed with saltwater, the rider then ready to swim the thing back out. Most little kids managed to get hold of a surfo – all they cost was a little bit of pocket money … and a few layers of skin, rashed off by the rubber! – and many shamed their parents by even standing up on the things.

These idyllic days in the Aussie surf were disrupted by the onset of World War II. Coastal beaches were fortified, crisscrossed with barbed wire and tank traps, and studded with coastal batteries and coast-watch observation posts. Many clubs went into recess, their members sometimes forming proxy surf clubs on beaches at the edge of war zones in Palestine and the Pacific. Back at home several clubs temporarily relaxed their membership regulations so that women could conduct patrols. After the war, women were still seen in carnival march pasts but they would not patrol surf beaches again for over thirty years.

TORQUAY PREPARES FOR INTERNATIONAL SURFING CARNIVAL

Torquay made last-minute preparations yesterday for the International Surf Carnival to-morrow—Australia's greatest surf and sand festival ever to be staged.

Bulldozers and graders scraped and pushed sand about the beach and in the clubhouse, officials tidied up as the day for the great event drew nearer.

But if the stage was not quite set, the players were.

Competing teams continued to arrive and surfers already established, trained in the water and on the beach.

Teams Drilling

At one stage yesterday Hawaiians, South Africans and West Australians were being put through their paces in rescue and resuscitation drill.

Further along the beach the crack New South Wales team carefully went through the finer points of surf drill.

Civic Reception

In Geelong yesterday, visiting surfers were welcomed officially at a civic reception given by the Mayor (Cr. A. L. Backwell).

At the reception were representatives of the United States, Hawaiian, Ceylonese, New Zealand, South African and Tasmanian teams.

Cr. Backwell said the eyes of the world were on Australia and it was up to Australians to make a good impression.

He described Geelong to the visitors and told them of the industries and the resorts.

Torquay the visitors cast speculative eyes over the scene of the carnival.

Was Cold

tative to South Africa and New Zealand; Jack McPhee, Australian Pat Manning, Australian beach sprint champion; Barry Tyson, outstanding New South Wales surfer; Barry Lawrence, New South Wales junior surf champion; Bill Clark and John Rodgers, New South Wales belt champion.

The team is coached by Lionel McDonald, coach of the Australian team at the 1954 Royal tour carnival and coach of the last two New South Wales teams.

Overseas Men

The overseas visitors include many famous surf men.

South Africa's Ernie Ricklan, one-time national pool champion, Don Coetzee, and board champion, Barry Edwards are also competing.

New Zealand have Paul Garrett, John Jervis, Jack Ryan and Duncan Long. New Zealand surfers won several events at the Royal tour carnival and are anxious for further competition with the Australians.

Interest In Boards

The Americans were particularly interested in the performance of boats and boards yesterday.

Manager Kirby Temple pointed out that the only surf board used at Los Angeles was a Glotter dory, manned by two rowers.

Americans also use a different type of board. It measures about nine feet, and is made of balsa wood coated with fibreglass.

In Maroubra, Frank Adler continued to popularise the hollow surfboard and in 1945 he formed the first organisation solely for board riders, the Australian Surf Board Association, but its members were still ostracised by the surf clubs. By now, board riders had perfected a specialised technique for steering their finless brutes. Called cornering, it required the rider to edge his trailing foot into the wave so that the increased drag slowly turned the board. But to corner in the opposite direction, the rider needed to change feet, a tricky manoeuvre on the narrow-tailed 'hollows'. With this new technique, surfers could finally angle away from the curl and head for the shoulder of the wave. But once caught by the whitewater, the board still took off for the beach sideways.

With the close of the war, beaches were stripped of their fortifications and by the following summer Australians were back in the water in increased numbers, only to be confronted by a new product of the atomic age: a revolutionary swimsuit – for women. While its impetus came from French fashion designers, its name came from a tiny atoll in the South Pacific where the United States had trialled the atom bomb in 1946. The new swimsuit was the bikini. It caused a sensation on Sydney beaches when it first appeared, but few women were game enough to be seen wearing one in public. The bikini simmered and sizzled away in the background of beach fashion until it really took off around a decade later.

So it was that Australia settled back into a cosy, conservative existence as the country rebuilt after the shock of war. Wireless and crystal sets beamed out crackly messages of soppy teen clichés set to music. Patti Page sang to us of Old Cape Cod. Johnny Ray told us of Little White Clouds, and the surf ski ruled the waves.

In 1951, the surf lifesaving clubs introduced a law that prohibited riding a surfboard unless you were a member of a lifesaving club. Bondi surfer Jack 'Bluey' Mayes caused a schism in the ranks of lifesavers when he formed a new club that was solely for board riders. The hundred or so new members who, as a result, deserted the lifesaving movement became known as the Cornel Wilde Gang. They grew their hair long, wore snappy 'Zoot suits' and ID bracelets and outraged the conservative elements of southside Sydney beaches. But slowly the haze of wowserism started to lift.

The kids born at the start of the war were just entering their teens and those born after the war were now fresh out of kindergarten. Ration cards and restrictions were now a thing of the past and the 1956 Olympic Games were coming to Melbourne. The country's first television broadcasts were about to beam and gleam into our loungerooms and athletes from all corners of the globe landed on our shores. Among them was a team of Californian lifeguards. Under their arms they carried the next big breakthrough in the development of surfing: the Malibu board.

⮕ It's a hot sunny Sunday in late summer. The vinyl seats of the Holden scorch your skin as you all pile into the back seat. Dad flicks his Rothmans butt out the open window, leans over and says … 'Hey kids, ya wanna go to Bondi?'

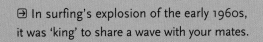
➔ In surfing's explosion of the early 1960s,
it was 'king' to share a wave with your mates.

The **Explosion**

THE SURFIES

They come from good homes.
They are well educated.
Why, then, do they turn
into common larrikins?

The Californian lifeguards were in Australia to compete against local life-savers in a series of demonstration carnivals held in conjunction with the 1956 Melbourne Olympics. Also taking part were teams from New Zealand, South Africa, Great Britain, Ceylon (Sri Lanka) and Hawaii. The Hawaiians and Californians brought with them long, sleek hollow paddle boards. But they also brought their new balsa Malibus.

Technological breakthroughs following World War II had eventually filtered through to surfboard construction, and postwar board builders in California combined the rigidity of the new construction material, fibreglass, with the lightweight timber, balsa. With these materials, they were able to reduce the length and weight of their boards – and simultaneously increase their durability.

Fellow Californian board designer Bob Simmons, who had also spent many years experimenting with board design, shot surf-riding from a sport of semi-controlled gliding into the space age when, after years of trial and error, he combined newly developed timber skegs with bottom curve, or rocker. The rocker lifted the nose of the board clear of the surface of the wave and also added turnability to the tail of the board. The skeg put an end to the sideways slide of the flat-bottomed hollow boards and redwoods. Surfers could turn, cut back and walk the board, right to the tip, while feeling the skeg holding them tight under the racing curl. The revolutionary surf craft was to take its name from the Californian point-break Malibu, with its cobblestone bottom and long peeling curl line, a perfect wave for the turning, trimming and nose-riding that the new lightweight and shorter boards allowed.

Shortish (3.5-metre) hollow boards with rudimentary skegs had appeared on our beaches by the late 1940s and some Malibu boards had appeared in Australia during the early 50s, with Hollywood actor Peter Lawford leaving a Malibu board at Bondi after

visiting Australia in 1952 and Hawaiian surfer Flippy Hoffman later bringing another to Sydney. Nipper Williams of Queenscliff had returned from Hawaii with a similar board and although Nipper would go on to become one of the country's leading board makers in the 1960s neither he nor anyone else seemed to think much of these little boards (around three metres long and weighing around twenty-five kilograms) at the time. Perhaps no one had seen what these boards could do when ridden hot-dog style.

'I'll give ya **two bob** for the works, mate!'
Australian surfer to visiting Californian Greg Noll in 1956 after sizing up the US team's balsa-wood boards

The potential of the new Malibu boards was eventually revealed at the demonstration carnivals, the first of which took place that November in Victoria at Torquay. The Torquay carnival was a real hit. Locals still claim there were over fifty thousand spectators; the same estimate was made by the local Geelong press at the time, while the Melbourne press placed the crowd at around twenty-five to thirty thousand people. Whatever the number, the beach at Torquay was clogged from the high-tide mark to the top of the scrubby dunes and cliffs with spectators, who watched the New Zealand surfers take out both the belt race and the surf team races. The Californians and Hawaiians were unplaced.

But the event was plagued by small surf and the visiting teams had no real opportunity to sample quality waves. However, late on Sunday afternoon, when the carnival

had wound down, some of the Californians went for a quick surf and snagged a couple of the tiny lefts that peaked and ran across Torquay beach. This session was witnessed by only a handful of Torquay surfers but they were so impressed with the boards used that, by the next weekend, local ski builder Bill Clymer had whipped up a hollow ply copy for them to try.

The Hawaiian team was led by Duke Kahanamoku, who was returning to Australia after an absence of forty-one years, while the lifeguards from California – Tom Zahn, Mike Bright, Bob Burnside and Greg Noll – were led by Tad Devine, son of another Hollywood actor, the perennial western sidekick Andy Devine. Greg Noll tells how their boards were given a thorough going-over by an Aussie competitor as they were unloaded from a flat-tray lorry. The Aussie turned to Noll and said, 'I'll give ya two bob for the works, mate!'

Noll must have been puzzled by the term *two bob*, but he had no doubt as to what the chap was getting at: as far as the Aussies were concerned these new-fangled balsa boards were worthless! For twenty years the local surfers had concentrated on developing boards designed for speed paddling and rescues but not performance surfing.

Noll was only eighteen at the time and had grown up in Manhattan Beach, part of a Californian surf culture already filled with weirdos and bohemians brought up on Kerouac. These drifting beach-side people spent the balmy summers patrolling the Pacific Coast Highway in Ford woodies or partying under beachside grass shacks with actors and starlets from the Malibu Colony, the sandy weekend retreat of Hollywood hopefuls. It was a far cry from the surf-club-dominated Australian beach culture in which the traditional highlight, once you were back on the beach, was 'the barrel': an eighteen-gallon keg of booze tapped behind the clubhouse after a carnival.

'.... but for those that have taken the gamble on a critical **take-off** and lost out can verify that extra knowledge of how to handle such a situation could prevent serious **injury** and mental anguish.'
Scott Dillon, Surfabout magazine 1963

Nevertheless, Noll took to the local beach scene enthusiastically and quickly fell in with the local lifesavers, who took him under their wing. Noll failed to join the rest of the Californians who, after leaving Torquay, flew straight to Sydney for another demonstration carnival at South Avalon. The Aussie lifesavers took him on a three-day pub crawl, all the way from Melbourne to the Harbour city. They showed him the pubs, the women and the incredible surf, but to his horror these lifesavers only hit the waves if there was a lifesaving club opposite the break! He finally arrived in Sydney unshaven, dishevelled and hung over. His head coach would have sent him home if he hadn't been such an important part of the team.

In the years to come Greg Noll would forge his reputation as one of California's first surf entrepreneurs, making surf movies to advertise his rapidly growing surfboard company while his fearless big-wave surfing earned him the nickname 'Da Bull' and a lasting place in surfing's pantheon.

Teams from each nation reconvened in Sydney. Once carnival duties were over, the visitors decided to hit the surf at Avalon and paddled out to a clean rolling left-hander at a spot down the beach known affectionately as 'Shark Alley'. Each of them had taken a few waves when one of the Yanks noticed a large crowd gathered on the beach. He paddled

up to fellow Californian Greg Noll and drawled, 'He-e-y Greg, there's a big crowd down there on the beach. I think someone must have drowned or something.'

'Maybe it's a shark!'

They each looked up and down the beach to see what had caused the commotion, but they could see nothing that explained the gathering crowd. In fact, it had been their display of hot-dogging that attracted the crowd's attention. They'd been angling, banking these little boards into hard turns and cutting across the waves, and walking up and down their boards. And they were smooth, controlled and graceful.

The young local surfers, who were stoked, swarmed all over the Yanks, eager for tips on how to copy this wild trick riding, this 'hot-dogging'. But some of the older surfers had other questions to ask: 'What's this bloody thing made of?' 'Where'd ya get this stuff from?' And, eventually, 'Hey mate, can I buy ya board?' And so, before the visiting surfers headed home, most had sold their boards to local surfers like Bob Evans, Peter Clare, Bob Pike and local hollow-board manufacturer Gordon Woods.

Stories of the unbelievable performances of these new boards quickly spread along the Sydney beaches and soon Woods and other local board-makers – Bill Wallace, Barry Bennett and Norm Casey – were inundated with orders for new Malibus … Orders they could not fill.

The large balsa flitches needed for Malibu boards were not readily available in this country and manufacturers often had to wait months for shipments to arrive from South America. The first large shipment didn't arrive until 1958. In the meantime surfers had to make do with hollow ply replicas, commonly called Ockanui boards.

When the balsa finally arrived, manufacturers then had to come to grips with the other raw materials: fibreglass and polyester resin. The technology behind the use of resin was still in its infancy, so board makers had to find out the hard way, using a well-known Aussie concept. This, of course, was the 'hit and miss' technique, blending just the right amount of 'hardener' with resin, which allowed the new batch to set and eventually cure.

The trick was figuring out how much hardener to add. One drop too much, and the whole mix would heat up and set too quickly, resulting in a tub of useless, hardening resin and a half-glassed balsa blank that needed stripping back to raw timber and starting all over again (provided there was enough blank left to work with)! Two drops too much and you had a 'hot batch', a glasser holding a smoking tub of rapidly hardening, spitting, bubbling goo, and another half-glassed blank! Three drops too much, and you had a fire – and occasionally, a charred factory!

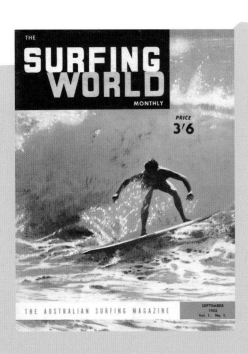

⬆⬈ The first editions. *Surfabout* folded in the late sixties but *Surfing World* is still published today.

The whole process was finally sorted out by Roger 'Duck' Keiran, who produced the first crude but effective fibreglass/balsa Malibus. But orders kept coming in and by 1959 more than 1500 balsa boards had been built throughout the country.

Orders kept coming in and by 1959 more than 1500 balsa boards had been built in Australia.

Small factories sprang up in Brookvale on Sydney's north side, while Vic Tantau, a competitor in the 1956 demonstration carnival at Torquay, was building balsa boards in Melbourne. In Brisbane an American company, Multi Form Plastics, was quick to follow. Their enterprise had little success but Joe Larkin on the Gold Coast and Hayden Kenny on the Sunshine Coast immediately took up the slack with their fledgling operations and quickly capitalised on the growing Queensland market. Dunlop Plastics also had a shot at board production, with their Pacific Star model of the mid-1960s, and Gill boards catered to the mass markets in the southern States. By then Hayden boards had a reputation as the best finished boards in the country.

In Brookvale, Greg McDonagh's was experimenting with styrene foam but the technology was still a bit dodgy. To 'blow' the foam, McDonagh had to be sure that the chemicals were mixed exactly and at a precise temperature. The new blend was then poured into a reinforced concrete mould. The lid of the mould was clamped shut and the chemical stew inside allowed to expand. It was like using a giant, lethal pressure-

⬆ A goofy-footer swings his board towards a smooth shoulder at Dee Why.

cooker. Too little of the blend, and the blank emerged light, fragile and useless. Too much blend, and the whole mould would blow apart and shower the factory with shards of foam and chunks of concrete.

Surfing had become the latest craze, one that newspapers, radio stations and a mysterious group of middle-class, middle-aged Australians known as 'the authorities!' lumped together with the Hula Hoop, Yo-Yos, the Pogo Stick and a disturbing music style that had been around for a few years called 'rock and roll'.

Thankfully for 'the authorities', it seemed rock and roll had already had its day and was on the way out. Its main protagonist, Elvis Presley, was in the US Army; black rock'n'roller Chuck Berry was in jail; and Buddy Holly, Eddie Cochran, Ritchie Valens and J.P. 'The Big Bopper' Richardson had all been tragically killed just as their rock careers were about to go into overdrive.

In California, American International Pictures were looking for something – any-thing – to fill the void and they quickly jumped on a new novel by Frederick Kohner. Kohner had churned out a slim, trashy paperback based on his daughter's summer vacation at nearby Malibu beach. Young Kathy Kohner had spent her summer vacation with characters like Moondoggie, Tubesteak and young hot-dogger Miki Dora, learning

'All I want is that some smart guy should make a **waterproof** transistor radio so that I don't **miss** the latest **surfing music** while I'm hot-dogging.'
Ross Giddings, Trump magazine, November 1963

NEW BEACH CULT

THE SURFIES

They come from good homes.

They are well educated.

NEW BEACH CULT THE SURFIES

They come from good homes

They are well educated

Why, then, do they turn

into common larrikins:

Leers, jeers, and whistles usually greet any girl walking by a group of surfies.
Posed by professional models.

They lie on the beaches joking about the squares who don't follow their weird cult.
Posed by professional models.

HE'S young. He's got money in his pocket. He lives in an upper-class suburb. He drives a car (either his own or his parents'). His hair is artificially bleached — generally with a well-known bath-cleanser or lemon juice.

He's a follower of Australia's latest and most baffling teenage cult. He's a "surfie" — sometimes known as a "Lemon Drop Kid."

Every fine weekend you will see him — and hundreds like him — at a surfing beach near a city, riding his surfboard and cracking a boomer as the big water comes rolling in.

You will look at him and think that he is a fine example of young Australian manhood.

UNLESS you meet him as his "other self."

Last week a Sydney North Shore woman met the "surfies" off the beach. She was holding a party for her 17-year-old daughter.

The invitations had been answered. The young girl's guests were enjoying themselves drinking punch and dancing when the roar of a dozen cars was heard outside the house.

Next moment a horde of young savages clutching bottles poured in among the party guests. The uninvited had arrived.

black stovepipe trousers which finished about four inches above the tops of their pointed black shoes, white shirts with extra-thin black ties, and black sweaters or jackets. The youngest were about 13; the oldest about 18.

An hour later they left the party in their cars, roaring off through the quiet suburban streets to another "show."

Behind them they left a shambles — smashed glassware and crockery, cigarette burns, a carpet with food and drink trampled into it, a ruined party, and a mother in tears.

Wrecking private parties is a favorite pastime

The "surfies" don't come from the wrong side of the tracks.

They attend good schools and are often G.P.S. pupils. Their parents are in many cases leaders of their social set. By all rights they have the ball at their feet.

But there is only one word for them — larrikins.

Crashing parties, bleaching

so-called good schools and "better-class" homes.

At weekends, when the weather is right, the "surfies" pick up their surfboards and head for the beaches.

They won't go with their parents. That would be too "square." Instead they prefer to hitch-hike from beach to beach on what they describe as a "surf safari."

At the beach they ride a few waves. Then they loll about on the beach with their girl-friends, squeezing lemon juice on their hair to help the sun bleach it at a faster rate, and

discussing where the latest "turn" is to be held.

As with most cults they have a vocabulary of their own.

Girl surfboard riders are called "gidgets," after a movie of that name. "Widows" are girls left sitting on the beach while their boy-friends ride the waves. "Sandies" are people who go on the beach but don't ride surfboards.

Saturday night is party-crashing night for the "surfies." They roll home around 2 a.m. on Sunday morning, more often than not drunk.

Startling facts? Perhaps. But they are facts which are now well known and causing an outcry from Perth to Brisbane.

Where do the parents stand in this rising tide of juvenile ratbaggery?

Many admit that they forbid their youngsters to go to parties — parties they crash — but the children openly defy them or say that they are going to a movie.

If they are chastised when found out, they retaliate by not going to school. In fact, playing truant to ride the boards is common practice.

Result: Worried but weak-willed parents are finding that the chances of their sons passing examinations are fading... and they are wondering why.

youngsters from nearby but not-so-select areas who oppose them.

These teenagers resent the "surfies" because of their better home circumstances and social standing.

And because they resent them they take up a cult which fosters affectations opposite to those of the "surfies."

Instead of bleaching their hair, the opposition movement pile grease on to it, so that even if it is naturally blond it is made as dark as possible.

Opposition

While the "surfies" effect dark and almost formal clothes the opposition — known as "Rockers" or "Hodads" — wear blue jeans and brightly coloured shirts.

Generally older than the "surfie," they devote their

⬆ No surf carnival was complete without the watery crash and bash of the surfboat race.

to surf, speaking the lingo and generally hanging out. Once back home she kept her parents fascinated (and most likely, horrified) with stories of all the strange characters and social misfits she met who spent their summers on the beach, waiting for the mythical ninth wave to carry them to teen heaven. The Malibu crew had given young pint-sized Kathy a nickname for summer. She was, they jived, 'a girl midget'!

Yep, she was Gidget.

The US movie house AIP took her pop's novel, whitewashed the story, grabbed Sandra Dee, teen heartthrob James Darren and Cliff Robertson and released the story as a new teen film.

Gidget, the movie, hit Australian shores at the end of 1959 and was the first in a series of AIP pictures to exploit the new craze, but local surfers weren't fooled by the corny characters and hokey plot, even if the surfing sequences did feature stunt work by some of California's hottest surfers.

Mainstream youth culture quickly adopted some of *Gidget*'s surf lingo and fashion but for dinky-die surfers the first movie to capture the imagination was a grainy, energy-charged 16-millimetre feature, *Big Wednesday*.

Mainstream youth culture quickly adopted some of the Gidget's surf lingo and fashion but for dinky-die surfers the first movie to capture the imagination was a grainy, energy-charged 16-millimetre feature, *Big Wednesday*.

⬅ An extract from *Everybody's* magazine, November 21, 1962.

John Severson's *Big Wednesday* premiered at Anzac House in Sydney in 1961. It was the first opportunity that most Sydney surfers had to check out the monstrous waves of Hawaii and the crowd went berserk. The giant surf, the huge crowd in the auditorium and the massive crowd locked outside had everyone stoked out of their minds, and, in a portent of things to come, things got – well – just a little bit out of hand. An Anzac mural hanging in the foyer was knocked to the floor and destroyed. 'The authorities' were not impressed and both the RSL and the SLSA were quick to condemn the loutish behaviour. And, of course, the more they condemned surfing, the more popular it became!

These first true surf films offered entertainment and more: they offered stoked little gremlins the chance to study the latest moves going down in the US and Hawaii. Magazines from the States were also filtering through, so finally the locals had something to copy – not just the latest flick turns, shoulder roll turns and nose-rides but hairstyles, fashion and music. By the end of that summer, kids on the beach were bleaching their hair with peroxide, or lemon juice, and pulling on long bermuda shorts and sloppy joes. Within twelve months of *Big Wednesday*'s debut, Australian surfers had their own surf magazines. Lee Cross fired the first shot with *Australian Surfer*, followed closely by Jack Eden with *Surfabout*.

The new magazines took up surfspeak like it was a secret code: full of *gas* duffle-coats, *king* boardies, *hodads* and *geese* from the suburbs, and *grouse heavies, tunnels,* and *pearls* which could all send you *down the mine*. But Cross's *Australian Surfer* lasted only six months before it fell over, perhaps because at the cover price of seven shillings and sixpence it was nearly twice the price of its rivals.

Bob 'Surge' Evans, who bought his first balsa board from Greg Noll in late 1956, chimed in with *Surfing World* in the spring of 1962. 'Surge' was already a fledgling surf entrepreneur and used his first issue of *Surfing World* to show what was happening in Hawaii. He had just returned from the Island State where he had been shooting his first surf film, *Surf Trek to Hawaii* and, having earlier had a huge success screening American Bud Browne's flick *The Big Surf* at Queenscliff SLSC, he ditched his jobs selling insurance and ladies' lingerie and went into full-time business promoting surfing through his magazine and movies.

The first Australian magazines concentrated on Sydney surf beaches, each of them running photographs of a young surfing pipsqueak who was the best hot-dogger in the country. Everyone on Sydney's beaches knew him as Midget and, although only in his teens, he had all the latest moves from the US down pat and was throwing in a few moves of his own. He was streets ahead of all the other kids and everyone knew it.

Suddenly it seemed that surfing and surfers were everywhere, even in Western

Finally the locals had something to copy – not just the latest flick turns, shoulder roll turns and nose-rides but hairstyles, fashion and music.

⬆ While top hot-doggers mastered the head-dip, some surfers took it a step further. Here's a body-dip at Kiddies Corner, Palm Beach.

Australia. The first hollow ply boards that had been dragged across the Nullarbor proved popular in the waves of City Beach and Cottesloe, some were even covered in ply and canvas. Chest boards, or paipos, were also common in the late 1940s and early 50s. Surf lifesavers had even tried out their toothpicks in the heavy surf of Yallingup as far back as 1956, but the first Ockanuis didn't appear in the West until the late 1950s, when someone got hold of an edition of Popular Mechanics that featured blueprints of a hollow board. When surfing went crazy over these boards, Perth-based surfers were forced to import them from Sydney and for a time Gordon Woods was able to keep up with the demand.

Perth surfer Brian Cole lived and worked in Sydney from 1958 until 1962, then returned with a couple of Barry Bennett surfboards. Shortly afterwards he started bringing Bennett blanks across the desert and even tried experimenting with styrene foam. He teamed up with Barry King and together they launched their new boards under the catchy label 'King-Cole Surfboards' only to find that business names that implied a 'royal' connection were not allowed. They settled on 'King and Cole Surfboards' and went into production, competing with Col and Rick Cordingley, Len Dibben and the Hawke brothers in the growing West Aussie surf industry.

Although the waves of Australia's southern coast are often chill and unforgiving, surfers in Tasmania first got into surfing in 1938, dragging their early surf-skis across the paddocks to Clifton Beach or Park Beach, or trying the marginally warmer waves along their north-west coast.

⬆ Surfari time – with an Austin Seven, a couple of balsa ockinuis, a guitar, and very hip facial hair.

Back on the mainland, as the craze took on epic proportions, some surf movies even made it onto television where they mixed it with the corny stateside television dramas *Adventures in Paradise*, *Hawaiian Eye* and *Surfside Six*. Surfers everywhere, inspired by the latest surf movies and TV shows and infatuated by surfing and all things American, grabbed a map and set out on 'surfari' in their trusty panel vans, Volksies and rusty station wagons, looking for the perfect wave.

The first destination was 'up north'. It was an obvious choice. Everyone knew of the warm clear water, sparkling white sand and abundant fishing waters north of Sydney. *Surfing World*'s first issue had already revealed a new break that was 'king' for bodysurfing *and* board riding. It was a tiny point near Yamba on the New South Wales north coast discovered by a bodysurfer, and brother of Bob, Dick Evans. Known as Angourie, this classy reef point was a real jewel and the first surfers who paddled out into its bowling, curling walls must have thought they had found heaven. It was heaven, but only for a few years. Before the decade was half over, the beaches south of Angourie were butchered – strip-mined for mineral sand.

To be honest, Angourie was a bit hairy. The waves broke over a shallow rock bottom and had punch – more punch than a lot of the early explorers could handle. For many, the first real discovery was just out of Kempsey, in the tiny coastal hamlet of Crescent Head. What surfers found here was a wave that broke in the true Malibu tradition. But it was longer – longer than anything along Sydney's beaches. And it was warm.

Photos started to show up, taken from the top of the headland above the break, that showed long, perfect walls fanning down the cobblestone point, and a roll of shots of Crescent was never complete without at least one that included the famous Crescent Head pandanus palm. Crescent, its line-up and its pandanus became the first icons of modern Aussie surfing. Like Angourie, it was heaven; and like Angourie, its southern beaches were soon to be gutted by rutile miners.

Crescent Head was the first of what became known as 'The Land of the Long Right Points'. Further north there were more of these luscious point waves: Lennox Head, Broken Head, and The Pass at Byron Bay. The Gold Coast had its own sub-group of long right points: at Snapper, Rainbow, Greenmount, Currumbin, Burleigh Heads and, at the top of the Sunshine Coast, Noosa Heads. Some were longer than Crescent, most were warmer and some were better, with faster, hollower sections, but for most surfers Crescent was the first stop on the road north. And although its reputation suffered when shorter boards took hold, its long, sunny curls defined for many the term *the perfect wave*.

The coast south of Sydney had its share of top-line waves too, but the colder water kept the pages of the magazines focused on 'up north'. Most of the south-coast reefs, ledges and hidden beaches were well off the beaten track and finding them needed patience and bloody good luck. One of the first to feature in *Surfabout* was The Farm just south of Shellharbour, but it wasn't a long way off the beaten track and was just another pretty beach break – something that the South Coast was peppered with. The real discovery was further down the coast at the end of a rutted sandy track signposted Lake Conjola. Up the beach and across a deep, sharky hole was a small island. This was Green Island, the first major discovery below Sydney. It was the country's premier left-hander until the end of the 1960s when it was overshadowed by a nearby break, first known as The Mechanism. For years The Mechanism was said to be too hollow and gnarly to surf, and it wasn't successfully ridden for another decade. By then the tag *Mechanism* was all but forgotten, replaced by a slew of names: Summercloud Bay, Torpedo Tubes, Wreck Bay and The Aussie Pipeline.

But the further south surfers looked, the colder the water became. Wetsuits – usually stiff, cumbersome skindiving suits – were uncommon. An old footy jumper with cut-off sleeves was cheaper, and a big fire on the beach cheaper still. The cold water apparently wasn't stopping surfers in Victoria. Stories were already filtering back to Sydney of Torquay, a coastal town west of Melbourne that had consistent but very cold surf. Apparently west of Torquay was another spot hidden by cliffs, where the heavies

'There was a time when the purchase of a surfboard was a **chancy deal,** an excursion to some small hidden workshop concealed by **mountains** of stacked **timber**...today one may drive to any one of half a dozen or so board shops.'
Surfing World, September 1962

← Brian Worth from Cronulla, at Green Island, the first major discovery on the New South Wales south coast. For a time Green Island was acknowledged as Australia's best left hander. Dave Milnes took this shot after wading out to the island at low tide.

→ UK surfer Gordon Burgiss watches as a monster set steams into Angourie. A wall of bush now obscures this view.

↑ Victorian big-wave surfer Terry Wall made his reputation at Bells in the early sixties, but in Easter 1965, he prayed for his life when caught inside by this monster set.

Big-wave surfing was a big deal. Magazines and movies were full of shots of huge Hawaiian peaks spitting out spray, boards and board riders.

really rolled in. Torquay Surf Club members had used their surfboat to gain access to this beach, until at the end of the 1950s a rough track was bulldozed along the cliffs to a gravel-sanded cove. Known as Bells Beach, this break had quality surf from two to twenty foot. Torquay surfer Peter Troy set up a surfboard rally at Bells over the January long weekend of 1962, when Glynn Ritchie hot-dogged his way through the three-foot surf and took home the first-place trophy and a one-pound note, his prize for the best ride of the day.

Big-wave surfing was a big deal. Magazines and movies were full of shots of huge Hawaiian peaks spitting out spray, boards and board riders. Accomplished Sydney surfers like Nipper Williams, Mick McMahon, Dave Jackman and Bob Pike had already tackled the huge Hawaiian surf, and Pike would later go on to conquer the biggest waves in the known surfing world. But it was Dave Jackman who made headlines in papers all over the country when, in 1961, he became the first board rider to tackle the Queenscliff Bombie successfully.

Jackman knew he had no hope of paddling out through the giant surf at Sydney's Queenscliff on that winter's morning so he drove over the headland to the next beach, Freshwater, where the surf wasn't so heavy. He punched through the shore break on his 12 foot 6 inch Rhino Chaser gun and paddled back around the headland before taking

his first wave at the Bombie. By the time he paddled back to the beach, he'd made head-lines across the country. Grainy front-page newspaper photos showed a grunting offshore peak scarred by a tiny line of wake. Jackman was barely visible, hidden by the spray in the trough of the wave.

Dave Jackman went back to Hawaii the following season. Also in Hawaii were Bob Evans and Midget Farrelly, Farrelly having returned to have another shot at the Makaha International Surfing Championships. The Makaha contest was regarded as an unoffi-cial world title and had never been won by a non-Hawaiian. Big surf didn't come to Makaha that year, and that suited Midget's hot-dog style perfectly. He impressed the judges as he picked off several waves and threaded his way through the notorious, back-wash-ravaged shore break. The judges could not fault this performance and Midget took out first place and returned home to find himself a hero. Coverage of his win was splashed across the front pages of newspapers around the country and he was inundat-ed with offers of endorsements, made guest appearances at dances and even compered his own surf show on telly.

The lure of the Hawaiian surf must have made a huge impact on two other Sydney surfers, Dave Chidgey and Bob McTavish. They were so impressed by the thought of the heavies that, in November 1962, they boarded the P&O liner *Oriana* and headed across the Pacific, unfortunately neglecting to buy tickets for the passage. They were finally sprung by authorities in Hawaii and five weeks later the stowaways were deported back to Australia.

Board builder and southside big-wave surfer Scott Dillon added to the big wave

'I'm sorry lass, but you can't wear that disgustingly brief bikini on my beach.'

mystique in 1963 when he conquered the Bare Island Bombora at the entrance to Botany Bay. But it seemed that Bells Beach offered the most consistent quality big waves in the country. Scott Dillon built a thriving surfboard business in Sydney, and staffed it with a bevy of top surfers and shapers. The Bare Island Bombie faded into memory and never featured in a surf magazine again.

As far as postwar Sydneysiders were concerned, Bells marked the boundary of the Aussie surf universe. Sure, some easterners had said that there were waves in a distant place known as 'The West' and apparently 'The West' was part of Australia (it even had a capital city, Perth). But no one in Sydney knew for sure whether there were real waves over there. It was possible that there was even surf in South Australia, but it was nearly as far away as the West, and if another place called Tasmania had surf, no one was game to brave the cold to go and find out. Even the great local beer was not a big enough incentive.

But things hadn't been going well in the Sydney surfing world. The Surf Lifesaving movement had become increasingly worried about the number of surfers jamming suburban beaches and escalating problems with loose boards clouting swimmers and bodysurfers. In 1960 the SLSA and local councils had banded together and introduced board registration. In that November on Sydney beaches it became illegal to surf a board that was not registered and did not bear the current rego sticker. Registration cost five shillings per year but was free if you were a surf club member. Of course, the fees went to the SLSA, as did the ten-pound fine that you copped if you were hunted down and caught without a current registration. Just to make matters worse, 'the authorities' confiscated the board of any offender.

In November 1960 on Sydney beaches it became illegal to surf a board that was not registered and did not bear the current rego sticker.

For a couple of summers, the beaches were like scenes from a wild west movie, as posses of clubbies, beach inspectors and police swept along the sand. Surfers with unregistered boards would scatter – some into the surf, from where they would paddle around the headlands to neighbouring beaches; others into the sandhills. Many would hurriedly bury their unregistered boards in the sand. It was a farce.

Surfing World magazine added some salient advice in the editorial of its first issue: 'Do not park across driveways, or leave your board on the footpath, or refuse to pay exorbitant parking fees, swear audibly or walk through private property.'

Local councils, not content with harassing surfers, soon turned their attention to the girls on the beach and invoked the by-laws of William Gocher's time. It seemed that girls were sunbaking on the beach while wearing indecent clothing. The clothing referred to was, of course, the bikini. Introduced over a decade earlier, it was already common on all Australian beaches, but where originally it had been a blousy cotton two-piece, new fabrics and lightweight boning had seen it become form-fitting – and brief. Too brief, claimed Waverley Council, south of Sydney. Beach Inspectors were instructed to enforce the by-laws, and any person wearing a swimsuit with sides less than two inches (5 centimetres) deep was liable to prosecution. The beach inspectors didn't carry tape measures but relied on a rule of thumb – two fingers' width! Laughingly, the arbitrary two inches' depth was duly enforced and in 1961 Miss Joan Barry was escorted from Bondi Beach in her 'lewd' bikini and fined three pounds. Not surprisingly, most young girls on the beach stuck to their guns, claimed the beach inspectors were dirty old men and wore even skimpier outfits to the beach.

In the water, things were just as chaotic. The SLSA clubs divided their beaches into surfing and non-surfing areas and often the best board-riding waves became off limits. Signs were posted along beaches showing each designated surfing area, leaving surfers sitting on the beach watching in frustration as strips of beach were enjoyed by a mere handful of swimmers while dozens of board riders were jammed into rocky beach corners.

Surfers at Freshwater Beach took things into their own hands and burnt the signs, or pulled them out, or bent them over at right angles. Eventually the local lifesaving club banned all surfing at Freshwater, but of course that didn't stop surfers from hitting the waves whenever the swell was up. Similar scenes were happening on all Sydney beaches and there was the odd bit of biffo.

You can imagine. You've wiped out and lost your board. It's washed down the beach and drifted into the shallows of the flagged area. You've swum two hundred metres through the rip and staggered up the beach only to be told that your board has

> **'Do not** park across driveways, or leave your board on the footpath, or **refuse** to pay exorbitant parking fees, swear audibly or walk through private property.'
> *Surfing World, volume 1, number 1, 1961*

been confiscated and you are about to be fined. Understandably, some surfers did their lolly!

It seemed that everyone was against surfers or their girlfriends: the clubbies, who were occasionally running them down with surfboats; the beach inspectors, who zealously enforced the flagged areas, confiscated boards or fined girls for wearing lewd bikinis; the police, who arrested them for surfing on unregistered boards; 'the authorities', who were happily taking the five-shilling registration and giving back nothing in return; and the newspapers, who had coined the term surfies! Heck, even other teenagers were after them.

These other teenagers were from the sweaty, land-locked suburbs and sported black leather jackets and denim jeans. They tucked packets of Marlboro in their rolled-up T-shirt sleeves and slicked back their hair with Californian Poppy. They were called Rockers. Or Bodgies (the boys) and Widgies (the girls).

For the previous five years, local rocker Johnny O'Keefe – 'The Wild One' – had stormed up and down the Hume Highway with his backing band The Deejays, knocking Bodgies and Widgies dead with gritty Oztralian Rock, but by the early 1960s O'Keefe's

career was losing steam, and his famed TV show *Six O'Clock Rock* was turning mainstream. For the 'slicked-down set' it seemed that rock music was on the way out, but the greasers weren't prepared to give up without a fight!

The newest sounds on transistor radios sprang from instrumental bands. The Ventures had just hit the big time with their twangy guitar hit 'Walk Don't Run' and Cliff Richard's backing band The Shadows racked up hits with the throbbing 'Apache' and 'F.B.I.' In the United States Dick Dale hardened the sound, added reverb, delay and echo and came up with Miserlou and the swinging sound of surf music.

Dale was followed by The Chantays with 'Pipeline', and The Surfaris with 'Wipe-out' and 'Surfer Joe'. Another Californian vocal group dropped the hot-rod songs from their repertoire, changed their name from The Pendletones to The Beach Boys and released their first hit record, *Surfin'*. They backed it up with 'Surfing USA' and name-checked Sydney's Narrabeen in the process. Within six months surf music had taken off. The Denvermen twanged up their sound and beat the rush to score the first hit when they came up with Aussie music's first true surf instrumental, 'Surfside'. The Delltones, the country's premier vocal band, hit the big time with their first surf hit, 'Hangin' Five', penned by a Sydney copper. Little Pattie shot to teen stardom with a real mouthful of a title singing 'He's My Long Haired Stompy-Wompy, Real-Gone Surfer Boy (yeah, yeah, yeh!)'. Even Robert Helpmann joined in, with his rather twee single 'Surfer Doll', as surfers took to summer dances up and down the Australian coast.

Although surf music had sprung from California, the Australian kids added their own element. It was the latest dance sensation, The Stomp, and again it was The Denvermen who were first to capitalise on the new dance when they released 'Avalon Stomp'. Roland Storm and the Statesmen followed up with 'It's The Stomp'.

The beauty of The Stomp lay in its simplicity. It didn't have the greased sexuality of The Jive or the raunchy precision of The Break. All anyone needed was a summer night, loud twangy guitars, a belly full of warm beer sloshed down in the sand dunes behind the surf club and the ability to count to two. Surf Stomps sprang up in surf lifesaving clubs and halls across the country. Stomp competitions took place at the Sydney Showgrounds and forty thousand Stompers took over nearby Lane Cove National Park for a radio station promotion. But the wildest Stomp in the land was in an old theatre in Kings Cross. It was Surf City.

Surf City showcased all the local stars and regularly headlined with local surf band

◁ The Surfies and Rockers War took hostilities right to the water's edge.

The Surfies and Rockers War

Most rockers kept away from Surf City, but they did hit the beaches, where they hung around on beach walls, swam in their jeans or tried to score with young sunbaking femlins. Of course, the surfers weren't going to stand for that and in early 1962 there were a few minor rumbles along the Esplanade at Manly. But the Bodgies came back the next weekend to settle a few scores and a wild punch-up followed, with the Rockers and Surfers going hammer and tongs right at the water's edge before the police stepped in. The newspapers lapped it up and named it 'The Surfies and Rockers War'.

The Surfies and Rockers War made front page news all over the country. Keen to get in on the act, the Queensland press and television stations took up the cudgels when police raided several Gold Coast hotels. What police found was drunken unruly behaviour at a poolside Pyjama Party!

The scene in Victoria was a little more subdued. It was too cold for pyjama parties and with the surf action taking place in small holiday towns at least an hour's drive from Melbourne, Rockers and Surfers rarely met head-on, and The Stomp only appeared at surf club dances over the short summers.

Melbourne itself was the centre of a jazzy beatnik scene in which the Jazzers copped a lot more stick from the Rockers than did the Surfers. Geelong, the nearest major town to Torquay, had its own 'Surf City' dance with its own share of biffo, caused when surfers down from Melbourne for the weekend upset local rockers by trying to race off the local girls.

The resort town of Lorne featured its own 'Stomp' in the local RSL hall, but tucked away under the cypresses on the foreshore was the swingingest dance of them all, The Wild Colonial Club. Surfers, Jazzers and Folkies all crammed in to watch the pick of the country's jazz and beat musos jamming away the summer nights.

Local Adelaide surfers had opened up their own dance venue, 'The Rincon', in West Beach Yacht Club. They loaded in enough beach sand to cover the dance floor of a hall licensed to hold four hundred people, then jammed in six hundred, turning away three hundred frustrated kids on opening night.

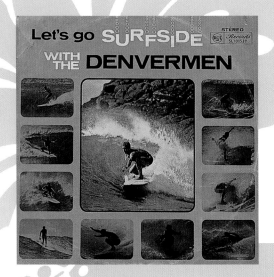

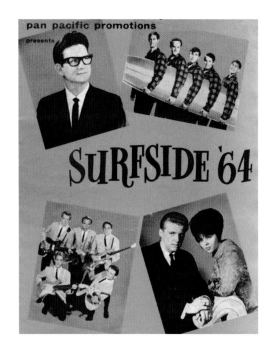

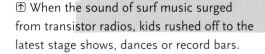

⬆ When the sound of surf music surged from transistor radios, kids rushed off to the latest stage shows, dances or record bars.

The Atlantics, who knocked the crowds dead with their big instrumental hits 'Bombora' and 'The Crusher'. Both tracks were huge-selling singles with a quality that equalled anything produced stateside.

Adelaide boys Hayden Burford, Ashley Waldeck and Peter Sutton had been bitten by the surfing bug when local lifesaver John Arnold returned to Adelaide with three Hobie-brand surfboards that he'd bought in the States. Arnold then turned his family shoe business into a surf shop and hooked up with Sydney manufacturer Barry Bennett. The locals tried out their first Bennetts in the gentle waves of Seaford and Moana and when these breaks went flat they headed for Goolwa and Middleton on the south coast.

In Sydney, Bob Evans was keen to conduct an international event held in Australia to rival the US's Makaha contest, but constant battles with officialdom stood in his way. Gathering a handful of like-minded surfing personalities around him, Evans put together the Australian Surfing Movement, which, by the end of 1963, became the Australian Surfriders Association. Its early office bearers included Evans and, with Midget Farrelly as President, it boasted representatives from board-riding clubs and surfing associations in all Australian States. Evans approached the petroleum company Ampol and convinced them that an Australian World Surfing Championship event could be successfully run. Ampol had already sponsored the local surf-riding titles and, even though surfing was still receiving bad press, the company agreed and Evans and his fledgling magazine set to work promoting the event. He finally got the event up and running in May 1964.

⬆ Panel vans and Kombis, parked in the quiet early morning shade in front of Miller's Pacific Hotel in Manly.

Along with Ampol, Evans enticed Qantas and Trans Australian Airways to act as co-sponsors. The airlines flew in highly rated overseas competitors Mike Doyle, L.J. Richards and Linda Benson from California; Joey Cabell of Hawaii; Gordon Burgiss from Britain; Frenchman Joel de Rosnay; Hector Velarde and Eduardo Arena from Peru; South African Max Wetteland; and Kiwi John Mc Dermott. Evans scored a major coup when the best Australian surfers and their overseas counterparts were entertained at an official function hosted by the Lord Mayor of Sydney.

Evans's publicity machine was in full gear and when the day of the final arrived the beach at Manly was chock-a-block with surfers, femlins, mums, dads and onlookers. His magazine *Surfing World* drew particular attention to 'the bright, warm, sun and gay atmosphere'. By the end of a weekend of competition, Doyle, Cabell and Richards had joined Australian surfers Bobby Brown, Mick Dooley and Midget Farrelly in the Men's Final, while Linda Benson was the only overseas surfer in an Australian-dominated Women's Final. Also in the water were Queenslander Phyllis O'Donnell, Victorian Gail Couper and Heather Nicholson from Coffs Harbour.

← Californian Mike Doyle, Midget Farrelly and Hawaiian Joey Cabell. Final placegetters at the first 'Worlds'.

The surf for the finals was small and well shaped and although Doyle and Cabell were renowned big-wave surfers, they were also top small-wave performers. But Midget was in his element. Midget's surfing had continued to develop. He threw in long, controlled nose-rides and a series of stylish slicing cutbacks. What he had picked up from the movies and magazines was now combined with his unique home-grown style and not surprisingly he won comfortably, with Doyle and Cabell in the minor placings.

'At the beach they ride a few waves. Then they loll about on the beach with their **girlfriends,** squeezing **lemon juice** on their hair to help the sun bleach it at a faster rate and discussing where the latest **"turn"** is to be held.'
Everybody's *magazine, November 1961*

Phyllis O'Donnell completed the rout with an equally impressive display of aggressive turns and stylin' soup rides, winning the Women's Final from Linda Benson and Heather Nicholson.

The beachside presentations created a media frenzy as thousands cheered each of the competitors in turn, and TV sensation and weirdo cult figure Mavis Brampston made a dazzling appearance on the podium in her trademark black dress and matching broad-brimmed hat.

For Evans it must have been a dream come true. The crowd on the beach on the day of the final was estimated at over 65,000 and television had broadcast the event across the nation. Using the funds and expertise of three high-profile companies, Evans had managed to coax the world's best surfers halfway across the globe to compete. Two Australians were anointed as world champions of what many thought to be a renegade sport.

No matter how you looked at it, surfing had become 'legit'.

← Midget Farrelly rides into first place and history in the first World Surfing titles.

⊡ By the mid 1960s Noosa Heads had
become the proving ground for Australian
surfers and board design. Noosa can lay flat
for months at a time, but when it's good ...
'it's like having a cup of tea with God'.

Surfing Goes Au Go-Go

The 1964 World Surfing Championships were a watershed for Australian surfing — a local lad had trumped the world's best surfers in the first world rated surfing event and had done it in front of 65,000 spectators but the contest effectively marked the end of surfing as a teen craze. The radio waves were increasingly filled with a new sound that replaced the twanging echo of surf music with the harmony and guitar hooks of Merseybeat and, just weeks after the contest, The Beatles arrived in Australia, sending teenagers all over the country into a frenzy. Beatle-cut hair replaced the peroxided curls of the wannabe surfers, Beatle boots replaced sneakers and 'Mods' became the latest teen tribe. But although surf music was dying, surf culture was not.

American International Pictures, chuffed by the success of *Gidget*, released *Ride the Wild Surf*. Quick to exploit Australian audiences, AIP included Aussie Olympic swimmer Murray Rose, who, as 'Swag Rielly', took a bit part beside Tab Hunter, Shelley Fabares and Barbara Eden.

Ride the Wild Surf became standard drive-in fodder for all young surfies, who coaxed their girlfriends into their panel vans hoping to catch a glimpse of some surf action before the windscreen fogged up completely.

American surf film producer Bruce Brown, after a couple of successful sixteen-millimetre surf features, took the formula, glossed it up, enlarged his best footage to thirty-five millimetres and released the most popular surf film of all time, *The Endless Summer*. When it reached Australian shores it went straight into mainstream cinemas, playing to packed houses wherever it showed. At Melbourne's Dendy Cinema it ran for six weeks straight.

Brown had earlier contracted local surfer Paul Witzig to shoot the Australian sequence. But the surf did not co-operate, so local audiences had to make do with some average footage of top local Sydney surfers Rod 'The Gopher' Sumpter, Robert 'Gnat' (later just Nat) Young and femlin Pearl Turton.

Meryon Sumpter, Rod's father, had been instrumental in the formation of the Australian Surfriders Association only twelve months before and Collaroy surfer

Gnat Young had taken out the junior events at the second Bells Beach contest and the world championships in May. But the lack of Australian footage was compensated for by the most memorable film sequence in surfing when the stars of the film, Robert August and Mike Hynson, along with Brown, *stumbled* onto a secret spot in South Africa. The spot, of course, was Cape St Francis – and it's unlikely that the surf there has ever been as good since.

Brown's footage of sparkling, flawless, four-foot surf proved that the perfect wave *did* exist. Coupled with Brown's witty script, fantastic surf action and a 'surf music *in excelcis*' soundtrack by The Sandals, *The Endless Summer* floored surfers and non-surfers alike.

By 1965 surfboard construction was big business. Barry Bennett had mastered the intricacies of 'foam blowing' and was supplying factories as far away as Perth with thousands of new blanks each year. Midget Farrelly, when he wasn't endorsing products such as the new Phillishave shaver, was endorsing his signature model skateboards which were produced by John Witzig (brother of film-maker Paul) and Gnat Young.

Production skateboards from Midget Farrelly's newly formed company and another Sydney-based company, Cooley, used tough timber decks and cast iron trucks, their wheels a composite of rubber and plastic, which made them quieter than homemade boards but not a lot safer. They were a great way to spend a surfless Sunday arvo, zig-zagging around Coca-Cola cans – provided you didn't mind Monday mornings back at work or school with an arm in plaster.

However, Midget wasn't letting his new business ventures keep him out of the water. In 1965, in small surf at Manly, he took out his next Australian title, followed by Robert Young and Bob McTavish. The women's event was taken out by Phyllis O'Donnell. In an impressive debut in the junior competition, Queenslander Peter Drouyn claimed the crown, but Young, now referred to as Nat, was ready to take over from Midget as the nation's surf hero. Nat didn't have it all his own way, though. In giant surf at the Bells Beach Easter competition of 1965, he had come up against the smooth surfing of Rob Conneeley.

The Bells event was becoming an unofficial Australian title and the surf on that Easter Sunday was big – very big! Giant swells thundered across the famous Bells Bowl, some sets stomping all the way through to the neighbouring break, Winkipop. Victoria's Terry Wall narrowly escaped drowning when caught inside by a set of waves that some experienced locals called eighteen foot plus, and some competitors hit the water with flippers tied to their boardshorts to help them on the long swim back through the Winkipop Express, the deadly rip common on big days at Bells. The women's event was cancelled.

⬆ John Quinn on a hand-made skateboard, or roller board. Look out for that pebble, Quinny!

Sidewalk Surfing One offshoot of surfing, the skateboard (or roller board, as it was briefly known), could be put together in your own garage. All that was needed was a set of wheels ripped from your little sister's roller skates screwed to a plank of wood shaped roughly like a miniature surfboard and measuring around 60 centimetres long by 15 centimetres wide. If your little sister didn't mind, it was because the skate wheels were steel and had already frightened the life out of her, skidding dangerously through any turns on your side driveway.

This new contraption was loads of fun on smooth footpaths and service station aprons – until you hit a problem, such as gravel. Even the tiniest pebble would lock up the wheels and send the rider head-first into the concrete. And then there was the high-speed wobble, which kicked in when board and skater hit Mach 1 while careering down the local hill of death. With high-speed wobbles, hitting the concrete was never an immediate thing; usually you had enough time to get in half a dozen galloping strides before the combined effects of gravity and terminal velocity took over ... then, and only then, did you hit the concrete.

Conneeley was already a surf star. He wrote a regular column for a Sydney daily, appeared regularly on television shows such as *Six O'Clock Rock* and featured in ads for the pre-Beatle hair cream, Brylcream. He was a comfortable winner in the big surf at Bells that year and Nat came in second.

Rob Conneeley's and Nat's battle at Bells were soon overshadowed by the battle that most young Australian surfers were about to confront with the Tory-led Australian Government which, under pressure from the American Congress, had agreed to provide aid to South Vietnam for its battle with the communist Viet-Cong. While Young and Conneeley were paddling out at Bells, an Australian combat force was preparing to leave for Vietnam. Just three months later, the Liberal Government introduced a ballot to conscript twenty-year-old males for National Service.

Surfers in their late teens were freaked out about being 'called up' and sent off to fight in a Vietnam war. Some simply refused to register and took off through Asia or lobbed for extensive stays at wave havens like Noosa Heads. Some surfers used their so-called 'surf bumps' as evidence of lingering, exotic bone diseases, while others came up with more inventive ways of flunking the medical to elude the draft. So one story goes, a southern surfer set out for the wilds of Wilson's Promontory where for two weeks he lived on baked beans and peanut butter sandwiches, abstained from washing, brushing his teeth and using toilet paper, then drove straight to the medical examination. Not surprisingly, his services were not required.

Despite not taking home the Bells trophy in 1965, Nat's hard turns and aggressive attitude were a contrast to the style that dominated US surfing and had filtered down to local surfers. This was the art of nose-riding – in the US it was now surfing's raison d'être – where time spent on the nose became the defining aspect of surf skill.

Concave nose-rider models became big business on both sides of the Pacific and at a later contest in California young Hawaiian surfer David Nuuhiwa made surfing history with a noseride of 10.6 seconds.

From 1960 to 1964, Californian surfer Phil Edwards had been acknowledged as the world's greatest surfer. Edwards had already visited our shores when he and Bruce Brown were shooting *Surfing Hollow Days*. Edwards' limp wrists and relaxed carving turns had become the benchmark for surfers around the globe, but even he was being overtaken by the emphasis on nose-riding. Tom Morey, a hot Californian surfer and design innovator, conceived a contest in which time spent on the nose was the only criterion in deciding the event's winner. Morey's event vindicated a design that featured a large concave running along the bottom of the board from the nose back to the midsection. Concave nose-rider models became big business on both sides of the Pacific

THE NEW WAVE '65

Surfers were still regarded as renegades but that didn't stop big companies using surfing and surfers to help promote their products.

Things Go Better With ... Surfing Surfers were still regarded as renegades but that didn't stop big companies using surfing and surfers to help promote their products. Among the first were Minties and Coca-Cola, both of which used surfing in their early television ad campaigns. TV surf shows were also succesful and several were around at the time — *Rob EG's Surfsounds*, which ran on ATN 7, and the ABC programs *Let's Go Surfing* (with Nat Young giving surfing demonstrations) and *The Midget Farrelly Surf Show*.

← Three surfers tuck their longboards under their arms and make the long trek, not to Cape St Francis, but to the waves at The Gardens south of Sydney.

→ 'Gnat' Young modelled part of his style on Californian Phil Edwards and also his mentor and, later, rival Midget Farrelly. Midget's influence is still apparent in this Easter 1965 shot of the Gnat at Bells.

SURFING WORLD GIRL

To the knowledge of "S.W." Tania Binning was the first of many girls to take up the Malibu board in Australia. A genuine surfboard enthusiast and a natural outdoor girl, Tania can usually be found on one or another of Sydney's beautiful north side beaches. Her base is Harbord but she follows the waves.

Surfing World Girl Aussie 'chicks' still weren't common in the water, even though Gail Couper, Phyl O'Donnell, Judy Trim and Tanya Binning were high-profile names in all the magazines. *Surfing World* still ran full-page shots of the Surfing World Girl, a monthly feature that owed more to *Australasian Post* than it did to real surfing.

Not many Aussie chicks were thrilled by a night at the local hall watching the latest surf film. As a rule they all followed the same formula: five-minute grabs of the hottest riders surfing local beaches, goofy humour, sped-up sequences, a handful of scripted gags, ferocious big-wave surfing, and the obligatory sequence of hideous wipe-outs, all washed down with a tropical sunset finale.

and at a later contest in California young Hawaiian surfer David Nuuhiwa made surfing history with a nose-ride of 10.6 seconds.

Now, both Nat and Midget could nose-ride, but it wasn't where Nat was heading and it certainly wasn't where the nomadic Bob McTavish was looking. After his brush with the US feds when he'd stowed away on the *Oriana*, Bob had ended up in Alexander Heads, shaping surfboards for Hayden Kenny and surfing the deserted point waves of the tiny coastal town of Noosa Heads. He sometimes lived on a diet of bananas and bread while experimenting with boards that were easier to turn and bank. It was a new style labelled 'involvement', and by definition it meant mixing it up with the whitewater. McTavish had become increasingly frustrated with the limitations of hefty straight-rockered boards that were so effective as nose-riders but not so good for surfing around the curl.

McTavish's new approach to surfing was evident at the 1966 Australian titles held on the Gold Coast. Midget looked fallible in the junky surf and could only take fourth place. The surfing press, now promoting the 'new era', wrote Midget off as a symbol of an era that had passed. Local junior Peter Drouyn won his second national title and Gail Couper from Victoria outclassed the other women competitors to claim the first of her many titles. Nat took the title and McTavish, with his new 'power style', took second place. McTavish lacked the polished style of both Farrelly and Young, but Bob wasn't looking for style per se; he was looking for something else.

The surfing press was also looking for something different, and that something was no longer Midget Farrelly. Writing for *Surfing World*, which had long championed Midget, was John Witzig, who took up some of McTavish's comments about functional surfing and painted the defeat of 21-year-old Farrelly as 'the end of an era'. Before you could say 'surf's up', Midget was out and Nat Young, with his new brand of power surfing, was in. It was like the change from the muu-muu to the mini skirt, with Bob McTavish as the fashion designer.

In 1966 Bells' reputation as the country's premier big wave spot was confirmed. Once again the Easter event saw spectacular 12-to-15-foot surf and clean offshore conditions. And this time Nat Young came out on top, with Victorian Terry Wall close behind. Up-and-coming junior Wayne Lynch was on his home turf and it was no surprise to anyone when he defeated Ocean Beach's Bill Monie.

The Bells event was also featured in the new pop magazine *Go-Set*. Launched by Melbourne scenesters Phillip Frazer and Tony Schauble and Sydneysider David Elfick, the fortnightly tabloid ran a regular surfing page which, in Melbourne, was compiled by Ian (later Molly) Meldrum. Discotheques and Go-Gos were taking over from the dying Surfstomps. Surfers were going go-go, with sun-bleached Beatle cuts, but getting into a fab disco dressed in a floral shirt, cords and gym boots had its problems. It was always the same story from the bouncers, 'Sorry fellers, we're full tonight. Come back next week. And wear a tie!'

Following the Aussie titles of 1966, Nat, Midget and Peter Drouyn, along with Gail Couper and Phyllis O'Donnell, were selected in the Australian team to compete in the next world championships, this time in San Diego.

The Americans were confident. Californian surfing was at the height of its stylish prowess, the local surfers trimming gracefully or swinging their Signature Models through slicing drop-knee cutbacks. In David Nuuhiwa, they had a surfer at the peak of his ability. Nuuhiwa was graceful and dynamic and could ride the nose like he invented it. Midget turned up with his new board, a shortish super-light stringer-less model, perfect for hot-dogging the punchy San Diego beach breaks. Nat brought along his favourite board, which he had nicknamed Sam. Sam was short too, and thin, with a deep raked skeg. Both their boards were shorter and thinner than those the Yanks were riding.

Nuuhiwa went out and went straight to the nose, but Nat went out and went straight for the jugular. He put Sam through his paces in the small surf, carving bottom turns and vicious cutbacks. When confronted by a section he couldn't get around, he went over it or grabbed the rail, pulled himself into a tight crouch and powered through the soup back up into green water, then hauled Sam back at the soup and repeated the whole shebang. Although Nuuhiwa comfortably took out the first round of the event, Nat won each of the subsequent rounds and went into the final with an insurmountable lead. Nuuhiwa didn't even make the final for one last showdown.

Nat returned home with another world title for Australia. He'd given the Yanks a flogging on their own turf – and destroyed nose-riding and traditional surfing in the process.

Midget made the final on his stringer-less board and took sixth. Rod Sumpter, the well-known Avalon surfer, took fifth, surfing a board sprayed with a replica of the Union Jack; he was now surfing for Great Britain, the country of his birth. Gail Couper, in her first internationally ranked event (strangely, the 1964 world titles did not qualify … there was no International Surfing Federation at the time) found the waves to her liking and came fourth on a count-back.

Nat's win prompted John Witzig to write up his account of the event and Nat's subsequent victory. It ran in the next issue of Australia's *Surfing World* and a rejigged version of the same article featured in the next issue of *Surfer* magazine, the bible of Californian surfing, but *Surfer* magazine gave Witzig's piece a new title: 'We're Tops

⊤ Picture sleeve E.P. for The Sandals' *The Endless Summer* soundtrack. Only the Australian and New Zealand pressings feature the blue sky.

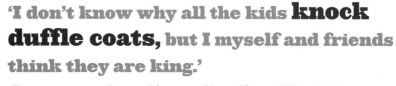

'I don't know why all the kids **knock duffle coats,** but I myself and friends think they are king.'
Letter to the editor, Surfing World, October 1965

Nat forces Victorian surfer Rod Brooks to chew white water.

'If you just **stand** on the **nose** from start to finish you've defeated creativity and **individualism** – the very essence of surfing.'
Nat Young, 1966

Roger Fallahey scratches over a monster at Bells in the Easter of 1965 – one of the biggest Easter surfs on record.

Now.' In the article, Witzig not only claimed that Australian surfers were streets ahead of the Yanks but paraphrased a remark from Californian surfer Bob Cooper who claimed that the US surfers were all pansies. Not surprisingly, American surfers were unimpressed. Not only had they been flogged competitively on their own beaches but the Aussies were less than humble about knocking them off. The Yanks didn't realise it at the time but within eighteen months their whole surf culture would be turned on its head by design developments from downunder.

The year 1966 also ended on a high note for The Beach Boys, who, with one of pop music's finest moments – the track 'Good Vibrations'– finally buried surf music, the genre they had helped build. This whirling sci-fi paean to high times started to drift across the surfing world and by the time the 1967 national titles were held, this time at Bells and at Easter, there had been a noticeable shift in perception – and not just in the water. Boards were like Sam: still over nine feet long, but lighter and thinner.

Unbelievably, Bells turned it on again, with more ten-foot surf. Nat put his increasingly aggressive style up against the cream of the new hot generation: surfers like

⊕ A young Wayne Lynch rides the nose in 1966. Three years later he turned the surfing world upside down with his vertical backhand surfing.

↗➔ A summer of Coppertone, Kreem-B-Tweens and paisley.

⬆ No barbie was successful without a station wagon full of longboards.

Victorian Wayne Lynch, Sydneysiders Ted Spencer and Keith Paull, dynamic Queenslander Peter Drouyn, newcomer Russell Hughes, and Bob McTavish. The women's title again went to Gail Couper. And once again Nat came out on top of the men's. Drouyn followed him, with Midget third.

◀ Peter Cornish on a Vee-bottom Stubbie during surfing's summer of love. The stubbie was shorter, wider, lighter and quickly obsolete.

In California, it was the dawn of the Summer of Love. The world was full of flowers, paisley, LSD and pot. The Beatles were putting the finishing touches to *Sergeant Pepper's*, while back in Sydney Bob McTavish was putting the finishing touches to a board design that would revolutionise surfing. Some years earlier Bob had met Californian surfer George Greenough, a professional fisherman visiting Australia to catch a few fish and go surfing. George was a true individualist, and although he came from a wealthy background, he could live on the smell of an oily rag, or could at least invent something useful from it.

'Have we become so **preoccupied** with the organisation and the side issues that they have become ends in themselves? Can **surfing** ever again return to those uncrowded days of **hollow** waves?'
Bob Evans, Surfing World, April 1967

George, like Bob, was passionate about surfboard and fin design, but the two differed in their choice of vehicles. George Greenough had hardly ridden a surfboard, instead preferring a kneeboard, and sometimes a surf mat – a modern version of the 1930s Surf-o-Plane. George had given his kneeboard a considerable amount of rejigging and had come up with a board he named Velo.

Velo was built almost entirely of fibreglass, with a small section of foam through the nose and rail to provide a minimum of flotation. Velo also featured a deep-raked fin that, like the rest of his board, flexed when pushed through a turn. The flexible fin and tail twanged back as the turn was released and snapped his red, spoon-shaped kneeboard

forward. McTavish quickly noticed that Velo and George were often slotted into the most powerful part of the wave, reaching places on a wave that a normal nine-foot board could never reach. These were places McTavish was trying to get to.

By early 1967, Bob and Nat, using George's ideas, were shortening their boards and adding the deep-raked twangy fins that George modelled on the dorsal fins of game fish he often caught. It was George who had fine-tuned Sam's fin in California before Nat took out the world title the year before.

But there were problems with building a board with flex like Velo, and although a few prototype flex boards were made, the problem was finally solved by adding a vee to the bottom of the board, allowing it to tilt onto a different plane as it turned. By the spring of 1967, a vastly different type of board was appearing on Sydney beaches. McTavish's model, produced by Keyo surfboards, was named the Plastic Machine. It was short (around eight feet long) and wide, with a deep flexible fin and a vee bottom that looked like the back of a cricket bat. Many boards based on this model were stringer-less and because of their full, blunt shape they were called Stubbies, Vee-bottoms, Wide-tails or Plastic Machines.

⊤ Absolutely classic Bells.

The 'involvement' style and the new Stubbies took surfing by storm. Models with flowery psychedelic names like The Crystal Vessel soon replaced the traditional long-boards in surf showrooms and sent some board builders in both Australia and California to the wall when they were caught with stands of obsolete and unsaleable Malibu boards.

The new Stubbies soon replaced the traditional longboards in surf showrooms and sent some board builders in both Australia and California to the wall when they were caught with stands of obsolete and unsaleable Malibu boards.

On the beach head, the short-board revolution was in full swing as boards lost more and more length. The Vee-bottom design was great in small, peaky beach breaks and floated over sections in the latest involvement manoeuvre, the re-entry, but in larger swells surfers were struggling to control the board. The wide stubby tail and extreme vee refused to bury into the wave face at speed. McTavish had taken a big wave-gun version

⊤ Another Peter Cornish, this time the Newcastle goofy-footer banks an 'involved' cutback at the 1967 Newcastle Contest.

of the Plastic Machine to Hawaii and paddled it out into some big waves at Sunset Beach. Every time he got to the bottom of one of Sunset's thundering peaks he threw his wide-tailed gun into banking bottom turns. Each time the board spun out; and each time that it did, Bob swam.

Following their stay on the North Shore, Bob and Nat turned up at Honolua Bay on the outer island of Maui. Although some of the local surfers were still riding standard-issue guns, some had jumped on their own local version of the shortboard and were using sleek racy Pintails. The spinout problems of the vee-bottom boards weren't encountered at Honolua and the spiralling waves were perfect for 'in the pocket' surfing. The Honolua sessions resulted in a cross-pollination of two surfing styles. While the Hawaiians were suitably impressed with the design capabilities of the Vee-bottom, the Aussie surfers were taken by the rocket-like speed of the narrow Pintail.

By the time the Aussies got home, the Stubby was dead. It had lasted a scant four months. Its offspring, the shorter Pintail, was out of date three months later and was replaced by the square tail shape, known as the Tracker, and its close relative, the round-pin Pocket Rocket, which dominated the waves of the 1968 Aussie titles held

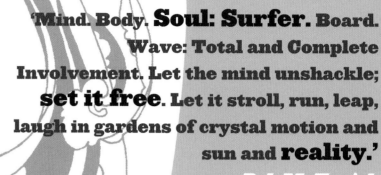

Surf International

As the dawn of Australian surfing's Summer of Love spread its acid-clouded haze over our beaches, another player appeared in the surfing media. John Witzig, who had penned the 'We're Tops Now' article, hit the newsstands as editor of a new magazine, *Surf International*. It was the spring of 1967 and *Surf International* was delivered by a newspaper taxi bursting from marmalade skies. The first local surf mag to be printed offshore, it was chock-a-block with colour shots and quickly became the voice of hippy surf consciousness. It hit just as the Plastic Machine took to the water, highlighting surfers riding the new Vee-bottoms and also showing them hanging on the beach, clad in satin Nehru-collar shirts and bandanas, with their girls in teased-up hair and mini skirts. Nat, McTavish and Midget also took time out from surfing to write some deep and meaningful pieces about the new scene. Bob McTavish captured the mood of the times in his psychedelic writings with passages like: 'Mind. Body. Soul: Surfer. Board. Wave: Total and Complete Involvement. Let the mind unshackle; set it free. Let it stroll, run, leap, laugh in gardens of crystal motion and sun and reality.'

again in Sydney. The event was won by Keith Paull.

Keith Paull's surfing was certainly eye-catching, a blend of smooth rail-to-rail turns and stylish trim, but many eyes were focused on the junior event, where a new star was emerging. This was Victorian surfer Wayne Lynch. Lynch had surfed superbly to take out the previous Aussie junior title at Bells in 1967, and once he hit the water, everyone realised that not only had he improved but he was doing things that no one had thought possible on a board. He was taking goofy-foot surfing to a new extreme with a repetoire of manoeuvres that no other surfer had managed to pull off so consistently and stylishly. By the 1968 Australian Titles he was taking his little rounded Pintail vertically up the face of the wave and re-entering at the top hitting turns with the fin barely holding into the wave and he was doing it on his back hand. He won the junior event comfortably and local girl Judy Trim took the women's title.

If it was hard keeping up with the progress in the water, it was just as hard trying to keep a handle on board design, as boards continued to shrink. Trackers and Pocket Rockets both quickly became obsolete as boards went mini – down to seven foot long by the end of 1968. For many recreational surfers who could only get in the water on weekends, it was the end. Some forked out the money for new boards that became obsolete before they could get them wet and once in the water many surfers faced a new problem. The little boards didn't float. Knee paddling became impossible and prone paddling

⊕ Paul Witzig's movie camera captured a few days that proved to be pivotal in the evolution of the surfboard. Here's Nat Young on a racy Vee at what became known as the Honolua Sessions.

The Honolua sessions resulted in a cross-pollination of two surfing styles. While the Hawaiians were suitably impressed with the design capabilities of the Vee-bottom, the Aussie surfers were taken by the rocket-like speed of the narrow Pintail.

The Swell of December 67

Although big winter surf is common in Victoria, it can occur at any time of the year, even in summer. A giant swell hit Victorian beaches halfway through December 1967. On Saturday 16 December, beaches all along the Victorian coast were closing out. On the west coast, Bells was unride-able, with fifteen-foot (four-metre) sets chopped up by a sea breeze that sent

surfers scurrying to protected 'once in a blue moon', mysto surf spots, like Fishos, that break only in a monster swell. The next day saw a drop in the swell, but conditions were still too rough for Bells and its neighbouring breaks. Conditions on open beaches closer to Port Phillip Heads were still treacherous, with twelve- to fifteen-foot close-out sets.

On that Sunday, 17 December 1967, at a restricted beach inside an Australian Military reserve just west of Portsea, a wetsuited body surfer decided to cool off and swam out into the surf. His name was Harold Holt and he was the Prime Minister of Australia. He plunged into the surf at Cheviot Beach, disappeared and, despite an intensive search, was never seen again.

wasn't a lot easier. Even surf bumps, the fibrous growths that developed on the knees and feet of board-riders as a result of years of knee paddling (and long a 'badge of honor' for true surfies) shrank and eventually vanished. Many surfers just gave up on the whole thing.

The shortboard revolution was no easier on the movie makers. Bob Evans's latest movie *Ride a White Horse* was released in major cinema chains in 35-millimetre format, but Evans had produced it as a 'greatest hits' movie, compiled from the best footage of his early movies – footage that was already obsolete. The movie bombed.

John Witzig's brother Paul, who had worked on *The Endless Summer*, had more success with his film, *The Hot Generation*. He kept it current by using footage of the young guns at Bells and used cuts from surf-garage band The Sunsets, who came up with the title track. *The Hot Generation* continued the idolatry of Nat Young and in one sequence showed Nat disappearing into a frothy tube at Bells and re-appearing as if by magic after the wave folded. But it wasn't magic, just clever editing. By splicing two separate shots together, Witzig cleverly heightened the impact of Nat's surfing.

Although *Ride a White Horse* had flopped, Bob Evans had another movie already in the can. His 1968 feature *The Way We Like It* gave Australian audiences their first glimpses of the Vee-bottoms, with footage of the 1967 Newcastle contest, and also highlighted Wayne Lynch's amazing surfing at the 1968 Australian titles. The distinctly Aussie soundtrack featured Tamam Shud who had started their career as The Sunsets and were now moving towards a jazzier, progressive feel.

Witzig's *Hot Generation* might have missed the short lifespan of the Stubbies and Lynch's performance in Sydney that year, but it proved successful enough for him to have another crack at movies and in 1969 he released *Evolution*. *Evolution* continued surfing's infatuation with Nat Young and added to it fantastic performances by Lynch and Ted Spencer, plus footage of a new break on the edge of the South Australian desert.

⬆ George Greenough on Velo at the Honolua Sessions, proving that a knee board could carve harder than a traditional board.

Blue Heaven

EVOLUTION

Parched and burnt surfers had been straggling back from the Great Australian Bight with tales of a fantastic clutch of surf spots where the desert met the coast. A place where it was always offshore and never flat, but (and this was a big but) the place was chock-a-block with sharks – large sharks and lots of 'em. Enough sharks for Steven Spielberg to send a camera crew to the area six years later to shoot underwater shots for his saltwater splatter movie *Jaws*. Although Paul Witzig got some great surfing footage in these waters, he was forced to release *Evolution* without the dynamic final sequence the film needed.

In May 1969 Australia's top riders dragged themselves away from their country soul existence — a lifestyle they adopted in quiet coastal towns, away from the crowded and 'plastic' city beaches. Despite their mumbles and grumbles about how contests were a 'bad trip' and lacked soul, many of the country's surf stars were happy to head off to yet another new wave frontier, this time in Western Australia, for the next national titles. Most surfers didn't have a clue what to expect, although for years rumours had grown about a surf spot with waves that rivalled Bells.

Evolution took surf cinematography into new ground. Its lo-fi feel was a radical departure from Witzig's previous film, *The Hot Generation*, and the polish of contemporary Californian features like *Free n' Easy*.

Its soundtrack, specifically composed for the new movie, used Tamam Shud, a rejigged version of The Sunsets. Their vocal tracks were a striking contrast to the instrumental cuts, provided by the free-form jamming of Sydney jazz-rockers Tully, who showcased an emerging Aussie Prog Rock movement. It was a daring choice.

Just as daring was the film's lack of narration, and when Witzig added his final sequence of Lynch at Margaret River, he backed it with Ravel's *Bolero*. Immediately, eight track cartridges of *Bolero* became *de rigueur* in Kombi stereos all along the coast.

But for *Evolution* the bottom line was the surfing, and it was hot. The film left audiences slack-jawed wherever it was shown.

◁ The Stubbie vee bottom was replaced by the streamlined round Pintail, or 'pocket rocket'. Bruce Channon rockets from the pocket at Seal Rocks.

The break was Margaret River, a brutal offshore left-hander that goofy-footer Wayne Lynch found ideal. He dominated the junior event with a display of vertical surfing and tube riding. Lynch's surfing at Margaret River gave Paul Witzig the climactic footage he needed and he quickly tacked a new finale onto *Evolution* and re-released it. Lynch's surfing saw him emerge as a genuine challenger to Nat's mastery and in many ways he was already surpassing Nat, especially with his backhand surfing. Both *Evolution* and Lynch quickly achieved a cult following.

But Lynch had a personal problem, namely the 'call up', and for three years he kept out of sight, only adding to his reputation and mystique. He surfed in the 1970 Aussie titles in Queensland, took out the junior title for his fourth consecutive year and gained a berth in the team for that year's world titles, scheduled for Australia – on Lynch's home ground of Bells Beach.

The previous world title event had been held in Puerto Rico in 1968 and had been won by Hawaiian old-school surfer Fred Hemmings. The Australian guns, Lynch, Spencer and Paull, bombed out early, and although Hughes, Farrelly and Young made the final, Hemmings' long conservative rides gave him the title. The women did no better and neither Gail Couper nor Phyllis O'Donnell advanced to the final.

With the concept of country soul really taking hold, hundreds of surfers were looking for a place where they could settle down with their old lady, grow their hair, grow their dope, hunt for magic mushies and make their own boards in their backyard shaping bays. Times were cosmic, as Mick De La Rue put it in a *Surfing World* piece in 1970 when he wrote, quite unashamedly: 'Spiritualism, metaphysical meditations and LSD all have a close affinity with waveriding inasmuch as they whittle down to, or blow up, the refined delicate movements, the unseen microscopic subtleties which are not judged or analysed due to their invisible quality.'

In 1969 George Greenough lashed out and bought a war surplus movie camera and turned to movie making, coming up with his first flick, *The Innermost Limits of Pure Fun*. With a cast comprising Bob McTavish, Russell Hughes, American Ritchie West and some little-known local surfers, Greenough highlighted the blossoming country soul movement, but *The Innermost Limits* also documented George's ability to film inside the tube while surfing.

With a handmade waterproof housing and camera strapped to his back, George stuffed himself into some serious tubes at Lennox Head. He must have taken some heavy

⬆ Teams in the 1970 World Surfing Titles march along Lorne's main street during the opening ceremony. Not all the US Mainland team marched, and like most teams the Hawaiians ditched the official team uniforms. It was a sign of the times.

The international teams were all housed in nearby Lorne and the Americans made headlines when one of their team members, staying in the Pacific Hotel, was arrested.

⬅ Midget on one of the racy Pintails that he helped popularise in his search for more and more speed.

beatings, but it was worth it. His closing sequence, 'The Coming of the Dawn', is shot as he rockets into the barrel, his camera grinding away in slow motion as tube after tube pounds away just above his head.

More and more surfers were becoming anti contest, seeing surfing more as an art than a sport that could be measured or judged subjectively. Nevertheless, the world's best surfers met again at Bells Beach in May 1970 for the world championships.

The US team was a blend of old and new faces and included David Nuuhiwa, who had relocated from Hawaii to California and achieved god-like status in the process. But the event lacked the promotional appeal of the 1964 titles, perhaps because the whole country was up in arms about Australia's continuing involvement in Vietnam. The Moratorium marches of the same May certainly took up a lot of press.

It also seemed there was a new force at work at Bells that year: the force of karma. Many hip competitors and most of the hangers-on were rapping about 'the bad vibes' that caused the event to be plagued by freezing weather and poor surf as Bells lay flat as a tack for nearly the whole event. The international teams were all housed in nearby Lorne and the Americans made headlines when one of their team members, staying in the Pacific Hotel, was arrested. The local press, particularly the conservative *Geelong Advertiser*, had a field day, and while the rest of the world was shuddering at the news that four American students at Ohio State University, who were peacefully protesting against their country's involvement in Vietnam, had been gunned down by the National Guard, the *Advertiser* chose to headline a story about an overseas surfer busted by local Geelong detectives for possessing a small amount of hashish.

The contest had got off to a bad start and the karma got so bad for David Nuuhiwa

'Spiritualism, **metaphysical** meditations and LSD all have a close affinity with waveriding inasmuch as they whittle down to, or **blow up,** the refined delicate movements, the unseen **microscopic subtleties** which are not judged or analysed due to their **invisible quality.'**
Mick De La Rue, Surfing World, 1969

⤴ Alby Falzon, *Surfing World* photographer, and Manly's 'Baddy' Treloar set out for Hawaii and a season of big surf on the North Shore.

⤴ Bob McTavish, who designed the Vee-bottomed Stubbie, developed even more progressive shapes as the decade closed.

Baddy Treloar carves his tiny single fin through the Bar Beach, Newcastle surf.

that he bailed on the whole thing. The event was finally completed at a secluded break ninety minutes from Bells known as Johanna Beach, which turned on some great waves for the occasion.

Midget made the final, along with Peter Drouyn and Nat Young, but for the Californians it was a case of sweet revenge. In the deepening shadows of the late afternoon gloom, Rolf Aurness, son of *Gunsmoke*'s Marshall Dillon (James Arness), claimed the title riding a longish Pintail. Midget followed Aurness into second place, then came Drouyn, Hawaiians Reno Abellira and Keone Downing and (in sixth place) Nat Young. The next day the women's final was completed at Skene's Creek, a little-known beach break just out of Apollo Bay, but no Australian women had made it through.

Many of the highly touted locals, including Wayne Lynch, had been caught out riding boards far too small for the conditions, some using boards in the sub-six-foot range. Finally, it seemed, boards in Australia had got too short.

The Aussies went back to their country soul to study their navels and dream about when they were 'tops now'. Aurness took his trophy and his Pintail, returned to California and, shortly after, dropped out of surfing and disappeared from the public eye.

Finally, it seemed, boards in Australia had got too short.

↗ Steve Jones slices through an oily wall at Burleigh Heads during the 1977 Efco Stubbies event.

↘ The sin-bin.

The New Counterculture

The Swinging Sixties slipped by before anyone had a chance to blink, as young people across the country experimented with a new counterculture and a new consciousness. Mind-altering drugs like marijuana and LSD offered many the chance to expand their minds. But for some, drugs offered only delusion and paranoia. The promise of a more peaceful world, despite the Beatles' karmic songbook, had not eventuated and even as the decade closed, Australian surfing lost one of its brightest stars when Cronulla surfer Bobby Brown was killed in a bar-room brawl. Bobby had been around since the start and was just hitting his peak. He'd placed at the first world titles and had starred in Witzig's *The Hot Generation*.

For others, the new decade offered a chance to experiment further with board design. Midget Farrelly flirted with the Sideslipper, a short, hard-railed flat-bottomed hybrid board, blessed (or, rather, cursed) with a tiny finger-sized fin. The fin was so small that the board slipped down the wave face, so that cutting back was no longer required. The Sideslipper would slide sideways with the curl and even spin 360 degrees, but its tiny fin offered no bite and as soon as the board was turned with any force it spun out.

At almost the same time, the surf grapevine carried stories of a newfangled super shortboard that was fitted with two fins. Boards with two fins certainly weren't new and had initially appeared in California as early as the late 1940s. American shaper Tom Hoye arrived in Sydney in 1971 with templates for these new wave-riding vehicles, which were short, thick and ugly, with two upright fins attached to the outer corners of their squarish plan shape. In small Australian surf they were great fun as they leaped about on the wave, shunting from fin to fin, but, like the Sideslipper, they spun out in hard turns or larger waves.

In Victoria, as in most things, the opposite was true, and boards appeared with long needle-like outlines, S-decks and long low-profile fins known as keels. Torquay shaper Pat Morgan made them popular in big surf, where they could really move out while carving long gentle turns. For a time both Nat Young and Wayne Lynch explored the potential of these boards but the keel was only at its best going straight and fast.

Although many young surfers set up alternative lifestyles in the Byron Bay area, for those in the southern States the promise of warm water was not as important as the consistent but colder swells of the Southern Ocean. In Victoria, Brian Singer and Doug Warbrick, two budding surf entrepreneurs, had been building some rough boards and operating a number of small surf shops. They finally set up base in Torquay and in the late 1960s opened The Bells Beach Surfshop. When the first Vee-bottoms hit, all covered in paisley and floral, they put their own slant on the Plastic Machine explosion by contracting Sydney board builder Shane Stedman, who had just released his Crystal Vessel model, and had him build their version, their lotus-bedecked Rip Curl Model. It wasn't long before they started building their own versions in Torquay, eventually setting up a factory in a disused bakery, even though competition in Victoria was already fierce, with Fred Pyke, George Rice and Klemm-Bell surfboards already dominating the market.

Shane Stedman's Sydney business was rapidly expanding. He'd set up a stable of the hottest surf stars in the country, including Ted Spencer, Judy Trim and Russell Hughes. Spencer's White Kite model and Shane's own mass market Pop-Out set him up as one of Australia's first surf moguls.

In Adelaide, South Aussie surfer John Arnold, who handled the local surf movie distribution, made a handful of early surf flicks and quickly established himself as that State's mover and shaker. He really hit the big time and signed Wayne Lynch to endorse the Wayne Lynch International Involvement model, a double-ended roundpin which appeared in all States and even across the United States. Arnold also picked up the Australian license for US-based O'Neill wetsuits. Until then, as mentioned, most surfers had taken to the cold water in footy jumpers or a White Stag tube suit or a Ben Crop beavertail vest. With Lynch's endorsement, Arnold released a flexible short-john that quickly took hold in the colder southern States.

This chilly combination of cold southern water and basic wetsuits gave Rip Curl's founders a great idea. Why not start making wetsuits in Torquay and tailor them specifically

⊼ Inside Kirra – before the 'Big Groyne', built to protect Coolangatta, killed the surf for nearly three years.

... all you needed to do was ride the tube with the entire inner rail of the board in contact with the wave face at the same time as the entire outer rail was in complete contact with descending curl.

Time Stands Still As surfers searched for the meaning of life and a way into the perfect tube of existence by using drugs and stoned-out metaphysics, some pretty wild ideas emerged. But none so wild as one that promised aqueous time travel. It was a cinch: all you needed to do was ride the tube with the entire inner rail of the board in contact with the wave face at the same time as the entire outer rail was in complete contact with descending curl (You Dig?) The board would then act as a conductor between two equal and opposing natural forces (Right On!) This would cause time to cease (Wow! Far Out!) and board and rider would float through the tube in a state of suspended animation! This idea was matched by that of an Australian champion surfer who claimed in a magazine feature that a new board felt alive for the first couple of weeks of its life because of a build-up of static electricity caused by electric planers and sanders. (Hmmm! Go on ...)

A reader with a quick grasp of the improbabilities of the theory quickly wrote to the magazine and pointed out that electricity is best conducted by water and that any build-up of static electricity would immediately discharge into the water the instant the board was wet! (QED!)

Freight free anywhere in Australia, two weeks delivery.

The only board that allows the surfer to ride sideways, backwards or in a spinning circle. The slipper has advantages a conventional board lacks. Speed comes easily, control is super positive through the flat bottom and low, soft rails. Basically, the board is slightly longer, thinner and diamond shape in outline. The fin is smaller to facilitate release only when desired. The rails and bottom allow a shallow draft fin in any case, and the fin used is both adjustable and removable.

Midget has ridden this shape in most every kind of wave. Reef surf was where the speed from the bottom and rails was best put to use. In beach break the board responded to all manoeuvres and created new freedoms with side slips to hold a curl position and 360's to fill the gap between the peaks of sections. Fantastic sensations can be had by riding whole sections backwards. The most average surfer is going to find this surfboard easy to ride. The side slipper can't be compared to any board that has gone before it. The only limitation this surfboard has is the surfer who rides it.

Farrelly Surfboards, 230 Harbord Road, Brookvale, 2108. Phone: 939-1724.

farrelly surfboards

⬆ Midget also flirted with Sideslippers.

↗ Grantley Oliver from the North Narrabeen brat-pack was a livewire surfer in and out of the water.

for the local market? Singer and Warbrick took a quick look at the surf movie market, decided that there were worse ways to raise some cash, and picked up distribution rights for a handful of movies, then used the proceeds to purchase their first batch of Neoprene. Based in Doug Warbrick's vacant block of old fibro flats, they set out developing their own wetsuit label, giving it the same name as their rapidly expanding surfboard operation.

In Sydney, surf journalist John Witzig was also on the lookout for a new venture, a format that would more accurately reflect the fast-moving surf culture. *Surfing World* was now printed offshore and the long delay between setting up each issue and that issue appearing on the newsstands was nearly three months. Witzig, fellow *Surfing World* photo-journalist Alby Falzon and *Go-Set* editor David Elfick got together and mapped out a new magazine that was part *Whole Earth Catalog* and part *Rolling Stone* and had the familiar 'now' feel of *Go-Set*.

Their new magazine, *Tracks*, plunged straight into leftist politics, and went gunning for rutile miners, bent politicians, the SLSA, crooked cops and anyone over thirty who sprang to mind. It also highlighted the activities of Byron Bay police, who were continually harassing anyone with long hair, searching their panel vans and Kombis or combing through their crumbling farm houses looking for dope. Byron Bay police weren't alone in their behaviour. The 'authorities' in every small coastal town were becoming alarmed as their towns were flooded with long-haired surfies … or even worse, long haired hippies … or worse still, long-haired surfing hippies who took Craig McGregor's advice when in 1970, he wrote in *Surfing World* this simple message 'Drop Out at Byron Bay, MAN. While there's still time!'

Long hair was in! So was cheese-cloth, denim, crocheted bikinis and patchouli oil. But unfortunately for surfers so was coastal development. It was at its worst on Queensland's Gold Coast where every available sand dune seemed ear-marked for a ten-storey block of flats.

The sand dunes were already under pressure, not from white-shoed developers but from erosion. In the early 1960s, on the State border of New South Wales and Queensland at the mouth of the Tweed River, large sea walls had been built to stabilise the treacherous Tweed River mouth and bar and in doing so created a new beach just north of the mouth. The new beach, Duranbah, provided great surf when the swell was too small to reach the points of Snapper Rocks and Greenmount but the new walls blocked the natural sand flow that replenished cyclone-damaged beaches immediately north of the walls. A series of major cyclones hit southern Queensland in 1967 and ripped apart beaches from Noosa to the Tweed, taking with them millions of dollars worth of caravan parks, front yards and motel swimming pools. Without the natural sand build-up, the beaches could not recover and more beach disappeared with every cyclone season. The worst affected beaches were Coolangatta and its neighbouring beach Kirra, along with Palm Beach and Noosa Heads. By the early 1970s all of these beaches were gone, leaving only wave-lapped boulder walls.

The point at Kirra was renowned for its great surf and its popularity had skyrocketed as boards shortened. Longboards were just too straight and unwieldy to tuck under the tube at Kirra but when tube riding became the next big thing in the early 1970s, the terms *tube* and *Kirra* became synonymous. However, the beach at Coolangatta had to be protected so council engineers decided to rebuild it by building a rock groyne at Kirra Point, trapping sand at Coolangatta Beach.

Coolangatta slowly recovered, but Kirra was now starved of sand. By the end of the next cyclone season the beach at North Kirra had disappeared and in the shadows of the new Kirra groyne, where one of the world's finest waves had once peeled, the water was now deep – and calm.

As beaches along the Queensland coast were disappearing, other breaks were being discovered. Queenslander Russell Hughes, following the hippy trail into South-East Asia, found himself on a small Indonesian island just east of Java. The place was a tropical paradise, complete with palm-fringed beaches, warm water, friendly local villagers and the first smattering of wandering hippies. Hughes also found a long curving beach full of great beach-break waves.

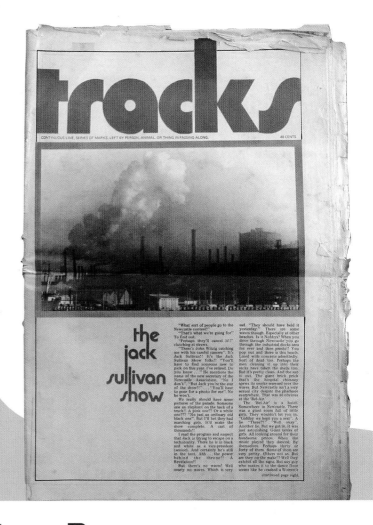

'Drop out at **Byron Bay, MAN. While there's still time.**'
Craig McGregor, Surf International, 1970

⬆ John Witzig debuted his new magazine, *Tracks*, without a surf shot on the front cover.

Back in Australia, the news of Hughes's discovery trickled down the grapevine to Alby Falzon, who had helped Bob Evans in his latest movie *The Way We Like It*. Falzon, working with *Tracks* magazine at the time, was also shooting his own surf movie. He learnt that the island was called Bali and that the surf broke just in front of a tiny village known as Kuta. It seemed a great place to film – a new discovery, tropical beaches and cheap accommodation – so Falzon teamed up veteran American surfer Rusty Miller with young Sydney surfer Steve Cooney and set out for the island of Bali.

The three surfers spent the first few days surfing the beach breaks at Kuta, relaxing under palm trees or exploring the island. Alby made a journey to a beautiful temple known as Ulu Watu, which was perched high atop a finger of land at the island's tip. And although back at Kuta the surf was small, Alby noticed a left-breaking wave along the cliffs below the temple. When the surf came up at Kuta a few days later, the three surfers set out to find the small left he had seen at the base of the cliffs. After hiking miles through rice fields they finally came to the edge of the cliffs and were amazed to find that the small left Alby had first seen was now a giant peeling tube that thumped below the cliffs, winding its way down the headland.

Stephen Cooney hadn't come expecting to find big surf and was riding a short single fin. Rusty Miller, a respected big-wave surfer, had his trusty semi-gun just in case, but neither surfer wore a leg-rope; these were yet to appear.

The island was called Bali and the surf broke just in front of a tiny village known as Kuta.

There were no steps down the cliff, and definitely no beach, just a small cave that tunnelled out to the surf at the base of the cliffs. Alby set up his movie camera and captured the genesis of a new surf destination as Rusty and young Stephen paddled into ten-foot-plus Ulu Watu.

Alby Falzon used the footage of this startling new discovery in his movie *Morning of the Earth*, released in 1972. His shots of Ulu Watu affected surfers the same way as the shots of Cape St Francis affected anyone who saw *The Endless Summer*, but for Australian surfers there were added attractions: Bali was warm, uncrowded, and right on everyone's doorstep.

Morning of the Earth perfectly captured the laid-back and zoned-out surf lifestyle of post-1960s surfers. Falzon heightened the movie's impact when he asked Sydney muso G. Wayne Thomas to produce the soundtrack. Thomas picked a select group of underground surf musicians in Terry Hannagan, Peter Howe and John J. Francis, added pianist Brian Cadd fresh from pop bands The Groop and Axiom, and reintroduced Tamam Shud.

Falzon also backed up Ulu Watu's debut with footage of Nat Young's long-lined speed surfing in perfect tubes at Broken Head and of two emerging Aussie surf stars. From Sydney came Terry Fitzgerald, fresh out of the urban ghetto of the North Narrabeen Boardriders Club, who took on the big Hawaiian surf of 1971 and built a reputation with a surf style based on speed, speed and more speed, later earning himself the moniker 'The Sultan of Speed'. And fresh from the dying days of the tubes of Kirra Point came Michael Peterson. Peterson's surfing blended Nat Young's aggression with Wayne Lynch's cutback jive; and at Kirra, Michael was king.

Morning of the Earth showed Michael riding flawless Kirra on a short squaretail board that looked like an ironing board with a fin, but did it wail! With a pumping left arm, Peterson would square off the bottom, pump his board under the curl and disappear into tube after tube, then emerge, fly up to the shoulder and carve back with a cutback

→ Michael Peterson pauses and lets the curl catch up at Kirra.

Adventures in Paradise

'Ulus' would become the first of the fantastic reef breaks to be discovered in Indonesia and for a time it challenged the Banzai Pipeline for the title 'best left in the world'. Little did Alby, Rusty Miller and Stephen Cooney know that just a couple of hundred yards down the reef was another left, Padang Padang, that was probably better. And on the other side of the island was a beautiful tubing right, the Sanur Pipe. It seemed logical: if Bali had waves, then there must be waves on the other islands of the archipelago.

Australian surf explorer Peter Troy bumped into two other Aussies, John Grissim and Kevin Norton, on board a steamer crossing to an island west of Sumatra known as Nias. On this island they found a palm-fringed cove that looked like it belonged on the set of South Pacific. On the outer edge of this cove, at Lagundi Bay, was a flawless right-hander. On other islands of the archipelago were more waves, and if you could brave the threat of tropical disease, giant snakes, tigers and third-world witch doctors, they were there for the taking.

← Padang-Padang, a grinding left-hand reef break in Bali, was one of the big discoveries of the 70s.

⬆ One ocean once covered the world, it was the ...

at full tilt. The Peterson full-tilt cutback took pride of place inside the cover of MOTE's soundtrack album and Peterson became the new darling of the surfing press.

Michael Peterson was a surfing savant. Shy, taciturn and withdrawn out of the water, he became a complete wave-riding animal the moment he got wet, and along with Terry Fitzgerald he quickly fought his way into the Australian national team as vanguard of a new tribe of surfing rough-nuts. But before Michael Peterson could book his ticket to the States for the 1972 world championships, again in California, he had another problem to face. He'd been busted.

Mind you, he wasn't the only top surfer lumbered with having too much fun with too much weed, but he was the current Australian champ, and the team's airfares were being partly sponsored by the Australian Government. Here was a classic conundrum for the Australian Surfrider Association, who were required to put the team together. Pick Peterson, the hottest surfer in the land and risk losing the sponsorship, forcing the rest of the team to find their own fare to the event; or leave him out, get the rest of the team to California courtesy of the sponsors, and face a revolt from ASA members?

Finally the ASA decided to include Peterson, there was no fallout from the sponsors, and the team set off for what was to prove to be the last amateur world title event for nearly a decade. The title went to little-known Hawaiian goofy-footer Jim Blears.

Although the world titles fizzed, 1972 ended on a bright note for many surfers when the Australian Government finally lowered the voting age from twenty-one years to eighteen – and simultaneously cut their own political throat. The new voters threw the government out, replaced them with Labor and thus put an end to National Service and Australia's involvement in Vietnam. The Labor Government's environmental policies spelt the beginning of the end for sand mining, and although it would take decades, our ravaged beaches started to recover. Suddenly, Australian society was shaking off conservatism and looking forward to an exciting future.

The [points for manoeuvres] concept attempted to remove subjectivity from judging by giving each manoeuvre a points value, with no consideration for style.

The Bells Beach Easter Contest was also looking towards the future. Rip Curl directors Singer and Warbrick saw an opportunity to increase their company's exposure by sponsoring the Bells Beach Easter Contest. Their business had ridden successfully on the back of the world titles at Bells in 1970 and both felt sure that a contest that offered cash prizes would draw a field of top international surfers into Torquay – and, hopefully, into their wetsuits. But this would change the event from an 'all comers' amateur event into a fully-fledged professional contest. For a number of years Bells did retain this 'all comers' appeal but there was a minor kerfuffle when Rip Curl insisted on renaming the event the Rip Curl Pro Championship.

Their event was modelled on a concept that 'Claw' Warbrick had seen in operation at the Hang Ten Surf Championships in Hawaii, called 'points for manoeuvres'. The concept attempted to remove subjectivity from judging by giving each manoeuvre a points value, with no consideration given for style. In theory it was simple; the most manoeuvres on the biggest waves scored the most points, and the surfer who wiggled and zigzagged the most, regardless of style, came out on top.

Michael Peterson made the trip down from Tweed Heads to take on the world's best at the new event. He read the system beautifully, wiggled and zigzagged more than anyone else, kept it stylish anyway, and returned home with the first place bell and a

POWER WAVE MODEL
for powerful and large waves

ALL WAVE MODEL
for small to medium waves

LEGROPES

⬅ Nah, it'll never work!

ROPES available

From Leash to Leg-rope

It first appeared inside the cover of an early *Surfing World*. A photo of a French surfer. Wearing a stiff beaver-tail wetsuit, he carries a hulking longboard under one arm. Around one ankle he appears to be wearing a dog collar. Snaking from the dog collar is a coil of fraying rope, its other end glued to the tail of the board. The caption for the photo reads 'Those French surfers are at it again. Don't try this in surf over one foot, and, don't try any spinners!'

It reappeared briefly in California as the 1970s dawned, only this time the cord was lighter; it was made of surgical rubber, not rope; and it was attached to the nose of the board by a suction cup. Called a 'leash', it was used to haul the nose of the board around as the surfer turned. It gave the surfer the added advantage of maintaining control of a board lost in a wipe-out. Provided you could live with the disadvantage of losing an eye when the board speared at you nose-first as the rubber leash snapped back, it seemed an interesting concept – nothing more. But the connection had been made. Why swim for your board, when with the right length of rubber, wipe-outs could be reduced to a mere inconvenience. The leash made its way to the tail of surfboards and in Australia was given the name leg-rope, goon cord, shock cord or just plain 'the leggie'.

Although the leggie took a little while to catch on (in Australian Surfrider Association contests, leggies were actually banned for some years), it eventually became as essential as board wax. More and more surfers flocked to the water, safe in the knowledge that their leggie would protect them at even the most dangerous breaks. There's no doubt that no other development in the history of surfing has done so much to cause crowded conditions as the humble leggie. No longer would surfers have to swim through cold, shark-infested waters to rescue their boards from fibreglass-ravaging rocks. Now beginner surfers could paddle out at the most hare-brained spots and take off, knowing that their leggie would save them a time-consuming and hazardous trip across rocks, and have them back in the take-off as quick as you can say 'twang'.

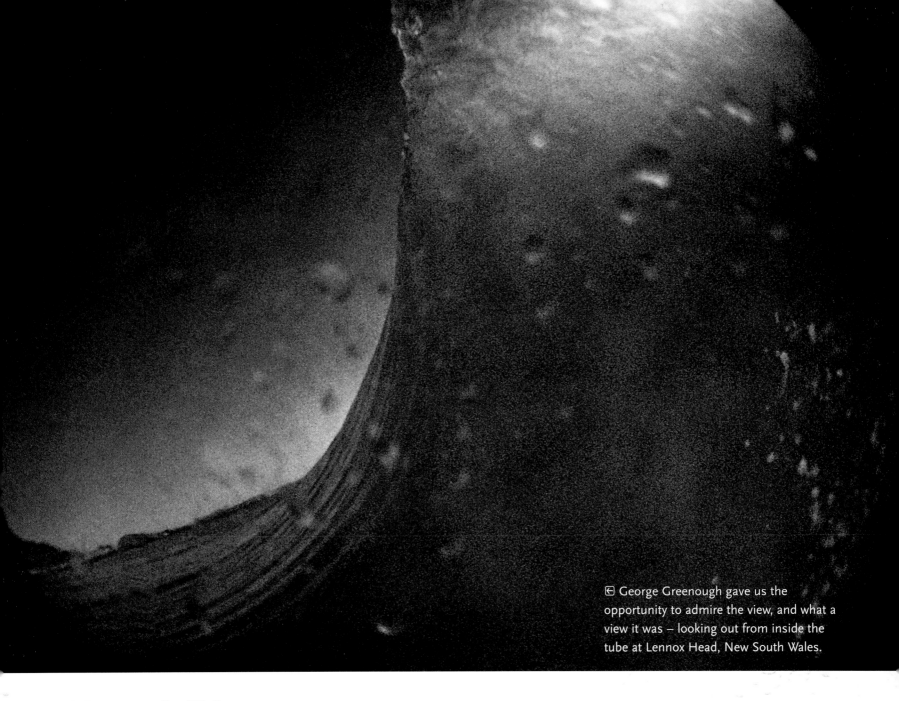

George Greenough gave us the opportunity to admire the view, and what a view it was – looking out from inside the tube at Lennox Head, New South Wales.

Echoes in the Tube

George Greenough found a high-profile international act to soundtrack his latest film offering. In a startling coup he was able to secure the rights to Pink Floyd's 1971 album *Meddle* for his short film *Echoes* that took over where The *Innermost Limits of Pure Fun* left off, with mind-blowing in-the-tube shots and classier editing.

Pink Floyd toured Australia just as George released *The Innermost Limits* and saw his film at a special screening in Sydney's arts co-operative the Yellow House. Two years later, in a serendipitous twist, George unwrapped a Christmas gift from his mother; it was *Meddle*, Pink Floyd's latest release. Its extended track, 'Echoes' seemed to fit perfectly with his new footage.

David Elfick, already working on a documentary that focused on George's unorthodox lifestyle, contacted Pink Floyd to discuss the project with them and before you could say 'dark side of the moon' George had 'Echoes' for his soundtrack and Pink Floyd had a brand spanking new print of his film.

The footage continued to feature in their light-shows until the 1990s.

Elfick's documentary of Greenough's lifestyle, *Crystal Voyager*, and the *Echoes* add-on premiered in 1973.

cheque for a thousand dollars. It wasn't Australia's first professional event, but it signalled not so much the birth of the professional era but the death of amateurism. Michael was looking forward to the challenge that the fledgling pro circuit offered. As he said at the time, 'I don't think I can be beaten out in the water, unless, of course, someone turns up who is better than me.'

Queensland surfers and Peterson were fast becoming the leaders of a new competitive push that threatened the decade-long dominance of New South Wales wave riders. This dominance had come increasingly from the surfers of North Narrabeen, a nondescript stretch of beach on Sydney's north side. What the beach lacked in architectural splendour it made up with waves.

The permanent sandbars at the mouth of the Narrabeen Lakes produce a top-quality left-hander and a better-than-average right, and their consistent quality has always attracted crowds – large crowds. The local board-riders' club built a reputation as fierce enforcers of the rule that local surfers get first pick of the waves – as well as second, third and fourth picks – and any westie (see definition) who snuck into the line-up to steal a few waves took their life in their hands.

The North Narrabeen Boardriders' regular contest season further entrenched their reputation, churning out a string of eager surf brats who joined the older regulars Terry Fitz, Dappa Oliver and Colin Smith. Yelping surf brats like Mark Warren and a big basic kid, Simon Anderson, were only too happy to take their urban surf style around the country – and around the world if they had to.

The Queensland push was just as strong and just as brash and it wasn't limited to Michael Peterson. There were the Neilson brothers, Paul and Rick, from Burleigh Heads, and Coolangatta grems Wayne Bartholomew and Peter Townend. Although a native of northern New South Wales, Peterson surfed mostly in the Coolangatta area, and he and Townend together with Bartholomew were often seen by the press as a triumvirate known as MP (Peterson), PT (Townend) and Bugs (Bartholomew).

The Neilsons already had Aussie titles and Hawaiian comps wins under their belts and were building an underground reputation as surfer–shapers and surf-wear retailers. The only other serious contender was Ian Cairns, a hulking blond surfer from the wilds of the west. Born in Victoria, he grew up surfing the powerful, lonely waves around Margaret River.

The Australian titles had returned to Margarets in 1973 amid controversy – not because of the outcome but because local surfers were hostile that a bunch of hotties from the east might come blitzkrieging along their beaches shooting photos of every surf spot west of Adelaide and return to publish the shots back east. Only ten years before, surfers had battled hodads and rockers, while welcoming visiting board riders. But by the early 1970s many surfers developed a mood of possessiveness, paranoia and isolationism when it came to 'their' surf spots. Called 'localism', this small-minded fanaticism was common in California and unfortunately it spread along our shores as well.

westie n. from surfspeak, person or surfer of low intelligence from western suburbs; see also bogan, Parra, hodad, touro, homie, bruce, dork, nerd.

'I don't think I can be **beaten** out in the water, unless, of course, someone turns up who is **better** than me.'
Michael Peterson, Tracks, 1975

⊕ Keeping warm, 70s style. This guy must have traded in the Afghan for something more panel-van friendly – a labrador and sheepskin coats.

Ugg boots, chunky knit cardigans and (for the boys) droopy moustaches were *de-riguer* Aussie beach style. Then pile everyone into the Kombi, Sandman or Drifter P.V. and head down the coast.

If you'd been in the queue to buy tickets when Crystal Voyager, Salt Water Wine or Fluid Drive showed at the Manly Silver Screen, the Brighton Town Hall, the Geelong Pix, Adelaide's Way Hall, or Brisbane's Ahlambra, you'd have checked out the rest of the dudes with their long, straight, blond hair parted dead centre, decked out in their flared denims, Kream shirts, and Crystal Cylinders T-shirts. The girls got down with the same hairstyle or a permed butter-fly cut, even more flares, chunky clogs that made some a foot taller – and, of course, a snug fleecy Golden Breed windcheater.

Golden Breed's moto-cross panelled crew wind-cheaters were the de-rigueur Aussie beach style when matched with Ugg boots, chunky knit cardigans and (for the boys) droopy moustaches. Then pile every-one into the Kombi, Sandman or Drifter P.V. and head down the coast with a glove-box stuffed with cas-settes of The Doobie Brothers, Neil Young, Jethro Tull, Zep and The Eagles and their Aussie clones LRB. Then hide the bong under the double mattress and throw Sasha the Afghan in the back to stand guard. Golden Breed was another business from the John Arnold stable which quickly carved out a niche mar-ket that was the envy of the other traditional labels Amco, Lee Cooper, Staggers and Saba. Arnold knew the value of sponsorship and endorse-ments, a lesson he'd learned during five years with Wayne Lynch, so he snapped up two of the world's hottest surfers, Hawaiians Jeff Hakman and Mr Pipeline, Gerry Lopez.

Lopez had been a little-known member of the Hawaiian team at the 1970 world titles but within two years he had achieved near god-like status, taking surfing towards Zen consciousness with his barrel riding of monster waves at Hawaii's meanest wave, the Banzai Pipeline. Lopez casually slotted his custom-built Lightning Bolt Pintails into tube after spitting tube with a style that influenced surfers all around the world, and wave-riders spent hours prac-tising the Lopez stance of 'standing limp in the eye' even if the surf was only three foot.

Shorter boards were attracting more girls to the surf, as was the surf mat, a long canvas version of the Surf-o-Plane that George Greenough had popularised. Many people saw these as great fun in sloppy surf and they were a perfect way to get your girlfriend out in the water.

Californian Tom Morey, the nose-riding contest innovator, had continued his experimentation with surf craft and was looking for something that filled the same role as the surf mat but without the hassles. Surf mats had to be inflated before each surf,

⊕ The Harmony Surfshop at North Kirra. A Gold Coast landmark, it was just the place to buy your silky boardshorts and your girlfriend's crocheted bikini.

Sorry We're Closed – Gone Surfing

In Torquay in the early 1970s, Rip Curl was expanding its wetsuit and surfboard business, but co-founder Doug Warbrick was trying to keep a level head on the whole industry when he told *Breakway* magazine in 1974 that he 'wasn't really interested in becoming a big business or executive or that sort of thing'.

Meanwhile a bunch of Rip Curl's mates were expanding a small clothing business that had started out making Ugg boots and sheepskin coats under the name Quiksilver. For three years, theirs

had been a small cottage industry that originally started in conjunction with Rip Curl, but the owners – Alan Green, John Law and Brewster Everett – branched out, making boardshorts that were proving popular as far away as Queensland.

Up north there was little competition, just a few backyard board builders and a handful of locals whipping up boardies for their mates or moving a little bit of stock from the boots of their cars in car parks and Saturday morning markets. Well-known surfer–shaper Gordon Merchant

'I wasn't really interested in becoming a **big business** or executive or that sort of thing.'
Rip Curl co-founder Doug Warbrick, 1974

and his wife Rena were selling more and more of their boardies using this method and had given their shorts and fledgling company a dinky-die Aussie name: Billabong.

they punctured easily and popped seams in hot weather. And the nipple rash they caused could keep you out of the water for days at a time.

Using a new polyurethane foam, Morey came up with a soft, flexible board that used a bevelled rail. Morey's board, known as 'the boogie' was only available as a DIY mail order kit, but it sold in ever increasing numbers. Morey knew he was onto a good thing and started producing 'completes' in his California factory and shipping them worldwide.

Greenough's flexi-fibreglass kneeboard, Velo, inspired other surfers to try out flex-tail kneeboards and although they were capable of deep turns and tube rides they only got going in premium-quality waves. Their flotation was minimal and riders had to contend with spending sessions virtually submerged, so most 'cripples' took to thickish blunt-nosed kneeboards known as 'slabs'.

Slabs coped with most wave conditions and riders like Dee Why's Peter Crawford took them to some extreme positions on the wave, but when boogie boards arrived on the scene slabs slowly fell from favour.

Surf mats and boogie boards were a fun alternative on days when the waves weren't up to scratch, but when the surf went downright flat more surfers turned to a new generation of skateboards. Like mats and boogies, these vehicles sprang from Californian surf culture and featured flexible fibreglass decks, high-performance trucks, bearings and wide polyurethane wheels that removed the danger of the stray pebble. The latest wave of surf movies often featured skateboard segments of blonde Californian skaters wailing in dry, kidney-shaped swimming pools.

Surfing was moving from being an underground sub-culture towards mainstream appeal. The Rip Curl Pro Championships continued to grow and prosper, and in Sydney, Coca-Cola renewed their love affair with surfing and sponsored their own professional event, the Coke Surfabout, first held in Sydney in 1974. Like Bells it drew a stellar overseas field and like Bells, the inaugural pro event was taken out by Michael Peterson. Peterson had by now racked up first places in three Bells events and the two Australian titles. Both pro events received television coverage but Peterson's win at Bells in 1975 caused a stir when he didn't show for the presentation.

The cameras were whirring when ASA president Stan Couper counted down the final placings and announced Peterson as the winner, but Michael didn't step up to the winner's table. (The early pro events weren't known for their pizzazz; the table was, in reality, a folding card table.)

A ripple of disquiet ran through the crowd. Stan repeated, 'Will Michael please step forward?' The ABC cameras whirred on, but still no show from Michael. Finally, from the back of the crowd assembled above the cliffs, someone called out saying they thought he was in Torquay, but no, he wasn't at Bells and the presentation ground to a halt. Couper and most of the ASA organising committee were furious and contemplated awarding the prize to the second-place competitor. The ABC film crew weren't exactly thrilled either, and producer David Hill went on to say, 'At least when I deal with cricketers they show up!' He was placated when it was decided to re-enact the presentation in the Torquay

⊤ Peter Townend perfected the 'soul arch' while working as a stunt double in the Hollywood surf-flick *Big Wednesday*. It later became one of his signature moves.

Morey's board, known as 'the boogie' was only available as a DIY mail order kit, but it sold in ever increasing numbers.

◁ Mark Warren swarmed all over the waves on his way to an Australian Title and a berth as an original Bronzed Aussie before becoming a media personality.

⊤ Peter Drouyn at Big Kirra. Drouyn is one of Australian surfing's forgotten heroes — well, if not forgotten, at least neglected. He had a stellar career as a junior, forged a career on the early pro circuit and also, courtesy of the Stubbies event, gave pro surfing the man-on-man concept. Did I also mention he once posed nude for *Cleo* magazine?

pub later that evening, and in a staged event Peterson finally did show to pick up his cheque and his Bell.

The new professional circuit had its problems too. It still used the amateur contest format, which, though scrupulously fair, could be unwieldy and not always spectator (read television) friendly. It took Queensland surfer and 'out there' visionary Peter Drouyn to tinker with the whole concept and come up with what he named the 'man-on-man' format.

Drouyn had started his surfing career in the 1960s as a brash, flamboyant junior. He had two Aussie Junior titles, an Australian Men's title, a world title finals appearance and enough pro contest results to give his proposal some credibility. He'd also flirted with an acting career and in the sexual revolution of the early 1970s, when women were still often seen in surfing magazine centrespreads, Drouyn turned the concept on its head by posing nude for *Cleo* magazine.

His new contest format reduced heat sizes from six surfers to two and, using a priority system, he allowed surfers to take turns catching waves. In 1977, he chatted up clothing company Efco, who made the popular but daggy Stubbies shorts, and they came on board as Number 1 sponsor, but his daring restructure of the contest format required one more thing to make it work – good surf, and he was in luck.

Burleigh Heads was blessed for a week with sunny conditions, offshores and flawless, head-high tubes. Crowds swarmed all over the headland at Burleigh to catch the Efco Stubbies contest action as the world's top surfers went berserk in the great waves. Drouyn must have been rubbing his hands together when the final came around, for it was Kirra surfer Michael Peterson, back on the circuit after a short hiatus, who emerged the winner.

'At least when I deal with cricketers **they show up!**'
ABC Producer David Hill, 1974

⬆ Stan Couper presents the trophies at Bells. Stan was responsible for taking a rambunctious and clumsy organisation, ironing out its kinks and twists, and guiding it towards professionalism.

Kirra Point had finally emerged from its groyne-induced slumber. The beach at Coolangatta had slowly returned and the overflow of sand gradually swept around the groyne and filled in the hole. A new sandbar also formed at the end of the groyne and lengthened the wave by another hundred metres. Although Michael Peterson was still the king of Kirra Point, by the time the sand returned he was immersed in a serious drug abuse problem and his days in the limelight were numbered.

Peterson's dominance in the water was soon overtaken by newcomers Wayne 'Rabbit' Bartholomew and Peter Townend. Both had graduated from the amateur ranks with top marks and had travelled to Hawaii early in their careers, keen to take on the newly formed pro circuit. Both were from the southern end of the Gold Coast and both wore the typical Queensland uniform of tanned skinny legs, knobby knees and blond hair. But their approach to surfing was markedly different. Townend was polished, poised, almost workmanlike in his approach. Bartholomew was flashy, spontaneous and

Captain Goodvibes, a.k.a. The Pig of Steel, was a cult figure in seventies surf culture. Why? Well, because this legendary pig rode deeper in the tube than anyone else. He also swore, consumed every kind of drug imaginable, fornicated with anything that moved, and viewed surfing as nothing more than a gigantic cosmic coincidence.

a bit of a lair. Both were a contrast to another Australian surfer who had matched them in his early years as a top junior competitor, but this gangly young kid came from Newcastle.

The grimy industrial city of Newcastle on the New South Wales' northern coast has its share of great waves and a long history of top-notch surfers, although some of them (like Sam Egan, Ted Harvey, Peter Cornish, Bob Lynch and Roger Clements) never received much coverage in the magazines of the day. The gangly kid with the twisted stance was Mark Richards. He had first sprung to notice when he appeared in Shepherd/Usher's short surf feature *Our Day in the Sun*, ripping up Angourie on an early twin fin, and he had already taken out the 1973 Australian Junior title.

By the mid-1970s he was firing on all four cylinders using a 'Stinger', a board design popularised in the islands by Larry Bertleman and Mark Liddell. Richards' style saw him nicknamed 'the wounded seagull', and although the tag was not meant to be a compliment, it seemed perfectly apt as he swooped and twisted his tall gangly frame into the most critical part of the wave.

Surfers for many years had copied the Phil Edwards style – a casual limp-wristed stance with elbows tucked in at the sides that was perfected in Californian point surf. But Richards threw his arms back and wide and cocked his wrists back, like a cop directing traffic. And he surfed with his knees locked together. As a result all his turns were made with the nose of his face near-buried in the water, the board on the point of spinning out. As he matured and the gangle of his adolescence faded, his surfing became a blend of the radical and the graceful.

Most top surfers end up with their styles copied by a bevy of less competent imitators. Richards' style was so unique that the imitators left him alone and homed in on copying surfers with more orthodox styles.

Richards, Terry Fitzgerald and Simon Anderson, all Australian title holders, were joined by Bartholomew and Ian Cairns as the vanguard of a new abrasive bunch of Aussie surfers who set out to make their careers from surfing. US surf commentator Drew Kampion labelled the group 'the yelping spawn of Kangarese'. It was an apt description as the young Australians went to Hawaii for the winter of 1975/76. Determined not to be cowed by the pounding strength of waves at places like Sunset Beach, Off the Wall, Waimea Bay and the Pipeline, their aggressive attack on the North Shore surf paid off and Richards, Cairns and Bartholomew took out the first three places in the Smirnoff Pro held in monstrous twenty-foot waves at Waimea Bay. Cairns backed up their combined victories with a first place in the prestigious Duke Kahanamoku Invitational.

Cairns then teamed up with Townend and another ex Aussie champion, Mark Warren and, with manager Mike Hurst, formed the Bronzed Aussies, a shrewd marketing tool that packaged the three surfers for promotional purposes. The Bronzed Aussies shared expenses, exposure and earnings, and launched a clothing company and a line of soft surfboards. The BAs also got about in a co-ordinated wardrobe that looked like it was left over from the set of *Saturday Night Fever*. But the plan failed to make impact and Warren bailed, replaced in quick succession by Jim Banks and Bondi hot-rat

'I want to go to **parties** and **hang out** with Bob Dylan and Jan Michael-Vincent and be **respected** by them on their level.'
Peter Townend, 1977

Too many pointy bits

The ASA was fighting a losing battle with the new pro circuit that was threatening the ASA's contest circuit, as well as one final stoush with 'the authorities', the SLSA.

The surfboard registration scheme of the early 1960s was finally laid to rest in 1968, but 'the authorities' thought they had one last ace up their sleeve, and they played it in front of the Australian Safety Standards Association, claiming that the modern surfboard was dangerous. Too many pointy bits, they claimed. Sending swimmers by the dozen to coastal hospital out-patient wards for treatment, they added.

The Surf Lifesaving movement proposed that all surfboards be of a standardised roundish shape and that each 'approved' board carry an approved sticker – and, further, that a fee be paid to have said sticker affixed. In an attack of 'dogs in the manger', they also claimed that the fee should be paid not to the ASA, the body that administered the sport, but to the Surf Lifesaving Association. The ASA appealed and produced a board made to the proposed specifications. Not surprisingly, it surfed like a dog and was so hard to control that it was even more likely to cause harm.

The ASA went on to win this battle when they produced evidence from every coastal hospital in the country that showed that injuries from stray surfboards were so few as to be non-existent. Eventually, though, the ASA lost out in the battle with professional contests. The Australian Championships circuit continued but with amateur status only, gradually becoming a feeder for emergent professional surfers.

Cheyne Horan. As a marketing tool, the Bronzed Aussies were probably twenty years ahead of their time, but to the surfing public the whole scheme smacked of hype.

Following the successful Australian assault on Hawaii in the season of 75/76, Bartholomew took a leaf out of John Witzig's book of surfing protocol and penned an article, 'Busting Down the Door', which documented the difficulties the Aussies encountered trying to gain respect from the Hawaiian contest structure. Like Witzig's piece ten years previously, it got people agitated – so agitated that on his next visit to Hawaii's North Shore Bartholomew ran into a bit of biffo outside a supermarket in Haliewa that left him without his two front teeth.

The loosely constructed pro tour took on more shape in 1976 with the formation of the International Professional Surfers (IPS), formed from an unholy alliance between Hawaiian and 1968 world champ Fred Hemmings, fellow Hawaiian journey-man surfer Randy Rarick and the Australian pros Townend and Cairns. The loose amalgam of pro contests spreading across the globe was gathered under the IPS umbrella and the professional world champion was decided using a ratings system based on event results. With a minimum of fanfare Townend claimed the first ever title, despite not winning a single event that year. Bartholomew, sans choppers, failed to make the top sixteen that first year, but after a truce was put in place with the Hawaiians he regrouped and fought his way back into the ratings, not finishing below fifth on the rankings for the next seven seasons and eventually claiming the title in 1978.

Despite the awkward beginnings of the pro tour, recreational surfers were fighting their way further away from crowded city breaks looking for waves – hol-

> 'If these **surfers** gave up their funny cigarettes and got stuck into **Resches,** this could be as **good** as Rugby League.'
> *Channel 9 cameraman at the Coke Contest, 1978*

low waves. The Lopez effect on tube riding had shifted the emphasis away from the smooth, long-lined waves considered 'perfect' in the 1960s. Crescent Head, Green Island, Bells and Noosa headed the list of spots that were now considered 'soft'. Burleigh Heads and Aussie Pipe now shared the limelight with Lennox Head, Winkipop and Kirra, but these spots were already being overrun with crowds, so surfers looked to the desert-fringed coasts of South Australia and to the reddened north-west coast above Perth.

Professional fishermen patrolled up and down this section of coast, the deckhands returning with wild stories of the unsurfed waves they had seen as their boats sheltered in quiet bays or behind islands. They told of barrelling left reef breaks, sharks, and the isolation of a desolate coast, and added they had a 4WD stocked with extra fuel, food and a quiver of guns, all ready to head into the desert when the fishing season was over. But few would mention just where they were heading.

⬆ Mick Peterson grew up in the warm waters of the Gold Coast, but a quarter-inch of neoprene rubber didn't stop him winning big bucks on the big fat walls of Bells.

The secrecy involved with one of the first discoveries, The Bluff, was so tight-lipped that when *Surfing World* ran a feature on the break, the photos were flopped, showing the break as a right-hander. But the word was out: somewhere up there, on the edge of nowhere, there were waves.

In 1977/78 Mark Richards had arrived on the North Shore with a quiver of revolutionary twin fins. The first twin fins had died in the early part of the decade but Richards was impressed by a tiny squat twin that Hawaiian Reno Abellira had used in the Coke Contest of 1976. Richards streamlined the shape and the new twin, with its canted-out, toed-in fins, was a huge improvement on the earlier versions. Although its small turning circle absolutely flew in small Aussie beach breaks, no one thought the boards would work in big surf, particularly on the North Shore. No one except Richards.

It's often said that a top surfer can ride a dunny door and make it look good – and a twin-fin's shape does have a lot in common with a dunny door – but Richards took his surfing to a higher level with the twin and proved its value in a wide variety of conditions. It worked so well for him that he took out four consecutive world titles, from 1979 to 1982. Although Richards' arch rivals were usually Rabbit Bartholomew or South African surfing superstar Shaun 'The Prawn' Thomson, in 1979, 81 and 82, the runner-up was Bondi surfer Cheyne Horan.

Bondi Beach, Australia's most famous strip of sand, has been a popular swimming hole for Sydneysiders since the late 1880s when it was nothing but a strip of sand dunes. Its snappy beach breaks bred a succession of top surfers, starting with Bluey Mayes, a flamboyant stylist who made the transition from a 1950s ski-riding clubbie to an early hotdogger in surfing's 60s explosion. Rob Conneeley and Kevin 'The Head' Brennan also made their reputations in the waves south of Ben Buckler headland. Kevin Brennan made waves the day he won both the 1965 NSW Junior and Senior Men's titles, and his stylish curl surfing had been a highlight of Paul Witzig's film *The Hot Generation*. But Bondi's reputation

> '**Mark Richards is also extremely fast and snappy and people don't realise how radically** he surfs. You have to see super slow motion movies ...'
> *Ian Cairns, January 1977*

was gradually tarnished by a deadly combination of urban decay and a vicious drug scene that devoured the soul of a generation of surfers. Ten years after Brennan's dual surf victories, he was found dead in Kings Cross. He was twenty-five years old.

Cheyne Horan first made his name as a top-notch skateboarder, and as a Bondi gremlin he'd also racked up impressive results as a cadet in the original National Schoolboys' Championships. His surfing closely resembled that of North Narrabeen's Grantley 'Dappa' Oliver: both shared a low centre of gravity and an arm-pumping bottom turn. Horan's cute looks and savvy image helped him into several Big M milk ads but belied his ferocious competitive nature, while his short stature never handicapped him in the big stuff in Hawaii.

Cute looks certainly didn't do teeny-bopper star Leif Garrett any harm when he burst out of Molly Meldrum's *Countdown* and onto the radio waves with his rehash of 'Surfin USA', which rocked the twelve year olds right down to their bobby sox. But luckily not all music was going bubblegum.

The punk boom of New York and London had briefly lashed Australia and created

◁ Mark Richards' unique style saw him nicknamed 'the wounded gull'. When he re-invented the twin fin the whole surfing world sat up and took notice. The wounded gull proved to be an ugly duckling and his surfing developed to be graceful, and still rad.

▷ An unidentified hottie zooms into the tunnel of love on the new Kirra sandbar.

↑ A line up of power-pop twin fins at Bob
Cooper's Coffs Harbour shop.

**The streamlined downrail speed shapes, all covered in
blue-green airbrush sprays of tropical island scenes and
cosmic sunsets, were traded in or thrown under the
house to gather dust. They were replaced by Richards-
inspired twin and single fins.**

an antipodean blend of new wave, hard rock and reactionary power-pop. The Bondi
Lifesaver, a slick and seedy cabaret in Bondi, showcased tough Aussie rock bands like
Cold Chisel and The Angels, while in Melbourne the equally seedy Bombay Rock saw
to the southern bands. One of these bands formed in
bay-side Mount Eliza when a bunch of Mornington
Peninsula surfers formed a new band. They were
Australian Crawl. They were no surf band, but their
audiences certainly were mainly surfers, at least until
their catchy pop-rock took hold all over the country.

This new wave and punk scene, with its uniform
of spiky hair and retro checks, zapped its way into
surf consciousness. The streamlined downrail speed
shapes, all covered in blue-green airbrush sprays of
tropical island scenes and cosmic sunsets, were traded in or thrown under the house to
gather dust. They were replaced by Richards-inspired twin and single fins, splattered in
funky red-pink, or black-white punk polka dots. The kids loved it. Especially a bunch of
kids from the north Sydney beach of Newport.

The board club that sprang up in Newport, known as Newport Plus, took over from
where North Narra board riders left off. They were another bunch of livewire kids, with
a rigorous contest format and a threatening presence, in and out of the water. Their local
break, a bog standard left-go-right-go-left again, was The Peak. Amazingly, The Peak was
a new surf spot that old Newport regulars claimed didn't exist in the 1960s. A series of
bomber swells hit the Sydney coast in 1974 and chewed the sand off the beach, exposing
the reef that formed this new break, The Peak. Apart from some seasonal variations, it's
been there ever since. The local kids didn't mind that it lacked the quality of Narrabeen;
it was consistent, and it was home.

⬆ Newport luminary, Derek Hynd.

This new, slightly upmarket urban surf ghetto was also home to a stellar bunch of punk-brats like the Carroll brothers Tom and Nick, Derek Hynd, Michael Twemlow, Rob Hale, Scott Lindley and 'soon to be a star in *Neighbours*' face, Peter Phelps. The 'plus' component of their club featured non-Newport surfers who were invited to join the club. Those blessed with an invitation to join included Bondi's Richard Cram and, later, Cronulla luminary Gary Green. Kingsley Looker from North Steyne was turned down when he tried to join; he didn't ride the right brand of board. The Newport Plus clique smacked to some of elitism, but Sydney beaches have always been controlled by tight local clans and this apparent elitism was nothing more than sophisticated territorialism. Looker, after a brief pro career, eventually drifted away from surfing and carved out a new career as a stylish pop-influenced pianist.

Sydney uni student and iconoclast Derek Hynd took his twin-fin attack into the pro circuit and made the top sixteen at the end of the decade. In 1979 Nick Carroll took out the Australian Open men's title. Nick repeated his success in 1981 and in the same year his little brother Tommy joined Derek Hynd in the top sixteen on the pro tour.

Tommy was short and nuggetty, built like a freckle-faced fire hydrant, and his surfing career, like Cheyne Horan's, was distinguished by numerous junior triumphs. Although similar in stature these two were like chalk and cheese – Carroll the up-and-coming goofy, Horan the contest-hardened natural footer; Horan blessed with good looks, Carroll

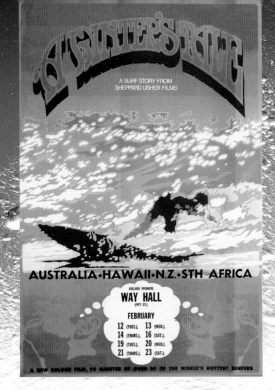

Surfing on the Big Screen

The surf movie circuit continued to bloom as surfers continued to drag their protesting girlfriends off to see the latest celluloid features. The highlight films from America had been Bud Browne's *Going Surfin'*, and McGillivray-Freeman's *Five Summer Stories*. Rod 'The Gopher' Sumpter, having settled in the United Kingdom when his competitive career was over, released *Freeform*, which had documented the 1970 world title final. His brother, David 'The Mexican' Sumpter, debuted with his rough-and-ready, atmospheric *On Any Morning*. He faced stiff competition from Shepherd Usher's *A Winter's Tale* and Bob Evans's film *Drouyn and Friends*.

After *Drouyn and Friends*' initial Australian season Evans took the film to the US. But tragically, while screening the film in a Florida theatre, Evans collapsed from a brain haemorrhage and died soon after. Australia had lost the man who had single-handedly kick-started the Australian surf media industry, setting the first world championships in motion and capturing the magic of Australia's early surfing history with his annual surf movies and *Surfing World* magazine.

The most impressive Aussie surf film of the 1970s came from Dick Hoole and Jack McCoy. McCoy had arrived in Australia with the Hawaiian team for the 1970 world titles. He stayed on, helping to set up the tabloid magazine *Backdoor*, and roamed the coast showing surf movies. He hooked up with Hoole, whom he had already met in Hawaii.

Dick Hoole had worked in early Byron Bay's surf factories, then travelled to the islands in 1969. Dick recalls sitting in his Honolulu flat above the Dewey Weber Surfshop when shop manager Randy Rarick returned, carrying the takings from a surf film he was screening in downtown Honolulu. Dick watched Randy tip the night's takings onto the kitchen table, sit down with a beer and start counting. It didn't take Dick long to realise there was more money in film-making than sanding boards or fixing dings. Back in Australia he and McCoy went into partnership, showing movies, shooting stills and planning their first film.

Halfway through shooting their debut film, they hit a snag. McCoy suffered head injuries in a skiing accident, and although the injury wasn't life threatening, Jack

suffered from amnesia. He couldn't even recognise his parents. But more significantly, at least as far as Hoole was concerned, McCoy had forgotten how to use the movie camera! Hoole-McCoy in conjunction with David Lourie eventually released *Tubular Swells* in 1976. The title was a cunning repositioning of Mike Oldfield's vinyl release of *Tubular Bells* but its US release saw a slight rejigging and it was released there with 'In search of' tacked on to its title, but regardless, its impact was not matched by that of American Bill Delaney's film *Free Ride*, released twelve months later. Sydneysider Steve Otton released his documentary style *Highway One* that same year and, although its hot surfing was backed up with a soundtrack that included Richard Clapton, Ol 55, The Dingoes and Skyhooks, it didn't gain anywhere near the popularity of *Free Ride* which featured the phenomenal tube riding of South African Shaun Thomson.

Filmed in ultra slow motion, the footage of Thomson's in-the-tube surfing soon found its way into several television ads and while he was visiting Australia for the pro season, Thomson found a sideline

as a male model. His movie star looks soon had him lounging under a coconut palm, being fed a Bounty Bar by a bikini-clad model.

When Bob Evans died Australia lost the man who had single-handedly kick-started the Australian surf media industry, setting the first world championships in motion and capturing the magic of Australia's early surfing history with his annual surf movies and *Surfing World* magazine.

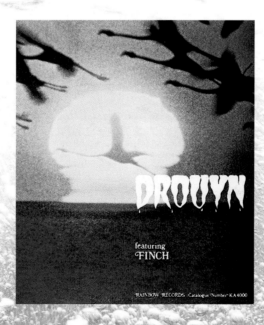

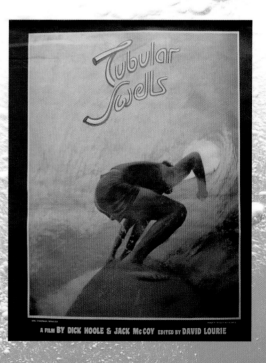

⬆ Gremlins became gremmies, then grommets, then grommies, then groms. Here's a bunch of them hanging out on the Gold Coast.

with a rusty crop of spiky curls; Horan, searching for a connection between spirituality and the discipline of surfing, and Carroll connecting beach suburbia with beckoning superstardom.

In nearby Manly, clanship was equally strong, as surfers from each block claimed dominance over the two-mile stretch of beach breaks – Queenscliff, North Steyne, Mid Steyne, South Steyne, Manly and the rocky headland of Fairy Bower – a stretch of beach clogged with all sorts of surfing humanity, from young rippers to old clubbies. Its 'dog-eat-dog' environment spawned one of Australia's unique surfing greats. Had she been born ten years earlier, Pam Burridge would have been labelled just another a 'femlin', but in the late 1970s that would have done her ability no credit. Simply put, she could surf as well as anyone else in the water.

Pam grew up in Clontarf but spent most of her teens conquering the tricky peaks of North Steyne. In her early teens, this lithe and determined goofy-footer was often mistaken for many of the other young hot grommets with their long hair blonded by the sun and surf. She surfed through local club events, found herself in the New South Wales State titles and surprised no one when she took first place in the women's event in 1979, 80 and 81, eventually becoming Australian women's champion in 1980 and again in 1981. By then she was well on her way to a long professional career.

Manly's 'dog-eat-dog' environment spawned one of Australia's unique surfing greats. Simply put, Pam Burridge could surf as well as anyone else in the water.

Finally, other young girls gained acceptance in the surf. In 1980 the Surf Lifesaving Association of Australia was forced to remove the shackles of male dominance when an Act of Parliament prohibited discrimination on the grounds of (among other things) gender. The Act allowed females to take the Surf Lifesaving 'Surf Bronze' exam, the surf bronze being the prerequisite for members performing patrol duties. 'Surf Bronze' holders could now become fully fledged club members, and the numbers of young girls patrolling surf beaches, and paddling Malibu rescue boards out into the surf, increased.

Just down the beach, at nearby Manly, surfers sometimes saw a hulking young chap shooting waves on the body. It wasn't just his size that caused the surfers to look up at him as they paddled out. This guy was bald – shaved bald – his glistening skull gleaming like a war-surplus torpedo as he bounced through the foam. The bodysurfer was a young uni student who played in a band with a handful of mates from the northern beaches, and their early gigs across the city made waves. Their music owed a small debt to punk and a small but significant debt to surf music. Proudly independent, they focused their attention on support for Australia's growing conservation movement. They called themselves Midnight Oil and their body surfing lead singer was Peter Garrett.

In the Oils' strident, political stage shows, Garrett, stranded amid hammering guitars, would dash about the stage like he had stepped on a live power cord, lecturing the crowd about untreated sewerage that filled the waves with filth and about the plight of indigenous Australians whose spiritual dreams and homelands had been snatched from them by white settlers. Their early single, 'Wedding Cake Island', took a more leisurely pace and was a true surf instrumental, echoing The Sandals' *Endless Summer* theme, Fleetwood Mac's 'Albatross', and Santo and Johnny's 50s mood piece, 'Sleepwalk'. But it was the strength of their live shows that carried them into the 80s.

The early 80s also saw the much awaited debut of Harry Hodges' second movie, *Band on the Run*, a surf-travelogue that featured pro surfers, Rabbit Bartholomew, Paul Neilsen and Brian Cregan. Hodge had released his first movie, *Liquid Gold*, in the early 70s, but it had made little impact. *Band on the Run*, which stole its name from the Paul McCartney and Wings album of the same name, had been plagued by financial problems and by the time it saw release, its surfing footage was out of date. Nevertheless, Hodge went on to make his name as a surf entrepreneur with the prestigious European arm of the Quiksilver label. Cregan founded Ocean and Earth, the accessories firm, and Neilsen, with his brother Rick built a retail empire with their Brothers Neilsen surfshop chain.

As the 70s sagged, the dominance of Midget Farrelly, Nat Young and Wayne Lynch also lessened. Midget, a design innovator, had popularised stringerless boards and needle-like pintails and promoted the first Sideslippers. He also explored the new worlds of hang-gliding and windsurfing, all the while building a thriving surf-blank business, and he re-emerged as a passionate roots surfer during longboarding's 90s renaissance.

'Surf Bronze' holders could now become fully fledged club members, and the numbers of young girls patrolling surf beaches, and paddling Malibu rescue boards out into the surf, increased.

Nat honed his promotional skills, then branching ever outwards, moved into the media and male modelling. In 1974 he was so impressed by the Australian Labor Party's environmental policies that he put his money where his mouth was and donated his third place prize purse of six hundred dollars from the 1974 Coke Surfabout to their election campaign. He also produced several surf movies and a series of surfing books. He too re-emerged during the renaissance of longboarding and took out four consecutive world longboard titles.

Wayne Lynch retreated from the circus of contest surfing to spend his time shaping boards and surfing isolated waves on Victoria's swell-wracked west coast. The more he shunned the spotlight, the more it searched him out, its cashed-up glare prying at his cult figure status. His last appearance in the top sixteen had been in 1976, the year before Townend, Warren and Cairns formed the Bronzed Aussies.

The BAs had seen pro surfing as an occupation, like pro tennis players and golfers who jet-setted around the globe plying their trade. The BAs would sell their jumpsuited surf skills to the highest bidder, but emerging punk new wave surfers of the late 1970s and early 1980s saw it differently.

⊡Nicky Wood, the youngest surfer to win
the Rip Curl Pro at Bells, blasts over
photographer Martin Tullemans at Duranbah.

Surfing Enters the **Mainstream**

By the early 1980s, the Rip Curl Pro at Bells Beach had become the most important event on the Australian contest calendar, and although for some years the surf had failed to deliver, the party circuit hadn't. Easter parties were all-night, 'last-man-standing' events and featured, in no order of importance, a loud, very loud, rock-and-roll band stuffed into a tiny lounge room, a bath overflowing with booze and a food fight. The night usually ended with some of the world's top surfers being driven home in the boot of someone's, anyone's, car.

Surf-wise, the Easter of 81 was different. The preliminary rounds were held in excellent head-high-plus surf at both Bells and Winkipop and by Good Friday, after four days of swell, the odds favoured the surf dying away by the time the final rounds were due to start on Easter Saturday. Only optimists said the swell would hold but Doug Warbrick claimed the swell was still building, leaving most pros to hit the hay that Friday night thinking, 'Sure, Claw, whatever you say!'

No matter what the pros were thinking when they climbed into bed, what most were saying on Saturday morning when they pulled into the Bells car park was, 'My God! Has anyone got a gun board I can borrow?' It was Big Saturday! Omigosh-sized, monster Bells! Sunny, offshore, fifteen-foot-plus Bells. The biggest surf for a pro contest outside Hawaii and the biggest Bells surf since 1965, and some old timers were saying this year was probably bigger.

Few pros had bothered to bring a quiver of gun boards so most spent the morning dashing around Torquay, dusting cobwebs from old guns stashed in back sheds. Those who couldn't get their hands on a gun had to make do with their everyday shortboards, some of which were twins fins and some as short as six feet. North Narrabeen's Simon Anderson caused some nervous chuckles when he walked down to the gravelly Bells sand with his six-foot-six Energy under his arm. Gasp! The board had three (yep, count 'em!) fins.

Anderson chalked up a steady stream of contest wins throughout the 1970s and into 1980, but while everyone else was wailing on twin fins, Simon just couldn't find a twinnie that worked. Probably the biggest surfer on the circuit, he had found that twin fins were too small to get him up and running, and contemporary single fins seemed too stiff. Around twelve months before the Bells event of 1981, Simon had bumped into local surfer and shaper Frank Williams, who was carrying under his arm what appeared to be a twin fin crossbred with a single fin. When Simon asked what the third fin was for, Williams told him that it stabilised the board, calming a twin's skaty feel. Simon thought the idea showed promise and made a handful of prototypes. He called them Thrusters, and adjusted the fin positions until he had them just right – and by golly, they worked. So he strapped a couple to the roof of his van for the long drive south to Bells.

The rumour mill was slowly spreading the news about Simon's new idea but a lot of people thought it was a gutsy move to paddle out at giant Bells and risk humiliation, and quite possibly drowning, just to try out a new-fangled board with too many fins. But Simon proved everyone wrong. He took off deep on monster after monster, laying his Thruster into deep bottom turns and carving off the tops. He proved his point, winning

Simon Anderson caused some nervous chuckles when he walked down to the gravelly Bells sand with his six-foot-six Energy under his arm. The board had three fins.

⊤ Simon Anderson puts his new three-finned thruster through its paces at North Narrabeen's Car Park Rights.

⊕ Cheyne Horan, The Lazer Zap and the
Ben Lexcen-inspired Star Fin.

the event comfortably. And when asked about the driving force behind his win he had the expectant media and boozy crowd in stitches when he explained that his win had nothing to do with the Thruster but was due to a combination of beers and snooker games in the Torquay pub. In his inimitable style Simon went on to explain, 'I was an average student – a bit below genius and a bit above dunce.'

It didn't take a huge leap of logic to figure out that a winged-keel fin designed specifically for surfing might improve a surfboard's performance.

He took the same competitive strategy to the Coke Contest in Sydney, and riding his Thruster again took out first place. To prove neither was a fluke, later in the year he took his three-fin Thruster to Hawaii and, on his backhand, won the Pipeline Masters. If he'd bothered to follow the circuit for the whole year, he may well have returned as the world champ. Within twelve months, every surfer on the pro tour – and not long after that, the whole world – was riding a three-fin Thruster. Everyone, that is, except Cheyne Horan.

In 1983, Australians had been thrilled by the success of John Bertrand, Alan Bond and Ben Lexcen in winning the world's most elitist yachting trophy, the America's Cup.

The success of the winning yacht, *Australia II*, had been partially attributed to Lexcen's secret weapon, a winged keel, and although *Australia II*'s winning margin, comparatively speaking, was not large, it didn't take a huge leap of logic to figure out that a winged-keel fin designed specifically for surfing might improve a surfboard's performance. Bringing together Lexcen's winged keel and the manufacturing prowess of Sydney board maker Geoff McCoy, Cheyne Horan planned finally to take out a world surfing title.

The new board, an ugly inverted-teardrop shape with a fat tail and spear-like nose, was designed by McCoy and known as a Lazer-Zap. Horan fitted the Lazer-Zap with Lexcen's keel fin, ignored the snickering media and rode it at the 1984 Rip Curl Pro at Bells. Like Anderson before him, he proved his doubters wrong, zapping his tiny wing-keel board across small, well-shaped waves to defeat young Newport surfer Tom Carroll in the final.

Although he took out the event, Cheyne's quest for a world title continued to elude him. Carroll's second placing gave him enough points to win his second world championship, while significantly, at least from the point of view of Simon Anderson, Cheyne's contest win proved to be the last time a single-fin shortboard would take a rider to victory in a major professional contest.

Onshore winds continually plague Australian surf spots, especially in the summer months. Along the eastern seaboard, the dreaded nor-easter hits late each morning, and along our southern shores wind shifts and southerly sea breezes can occur at any time but seem mostly to spring up just as you're about to hit the water. In the west, the Fremantle Doctor clocks on no later than mid-morning. So, what to do for the rest of the day? Once upon a time, surfers had made up their own extreme sports, most of which involved jumping off something high into something wet! The hairiest spots were Sydney's Warriewood Drop, The Banana State's Hells Gates, Woppa Dam, and Currumbin Rockslide, Victoria's chilly Erskine River Rapids, Moorooduc Quarry jump, and the Devilbend Reservoir slide.

Less death-defying than leaping off rocks, though just as much fun, was the Hobie Cat, a fibre-glass catamaran built specifically to surf unbroken swells. Designed by Californian board maker Hobie Alter, the Hobie Cat was a streamlined relative of the plywood Quick Cat, which was a common sight in the surf at Kirra, and 'Hobies' and the smaller 'Surf Cats' became a popular but expensive alternative during the 1970s and early 80s.

The biggest breakthrough for wind-swept afternoons, however, was the

⊤ Throughout the 70s and early 80s, the names Terry Richardson and Wreck Bay went hand in glove. Here's Terry, snugly slipping into a Wreck Bay tube.

'You'd have to be the **world's best** surfer to make a living out of it. There's no way of making a steady **income** out of it.'
Tom Carroll, 1977

Puberty Blues

Mainstream Australian cinema had a crack at the beach culture genre in 1981 when Gabrielle Carey and Kathy Lette's novel, *Puberty Blues*, was brought to the silver screen by Bruce Beresford. Lette and Carey took teen beach culture and looked at it through the eyes of the teenage girls who hung at Sydney's Cronulla Beach. What *Puberty Blues* revealed (not surprisingly) was a chauvinist beach culture that crammed girls into bikinis, the back of the panel van, and the tacky side of a male-dominated surf culture. Many surfers continued to see themselves as caring, sharing, liberal-minded, New Age men. *Puberty Blues* made the point that the caring and sharing didn't apply unless the girls were disrobing in the back of a HR Holden panel van. It was a point made by a *Tracks* reader identifying themselves only as Randy Sandy in a letter to the editor: 'I've got nothing against virgins, after all, I used to be one myself!'

Storm Riders

The exploding windsurfing scene was highlighted in David Lourie, Dick Hoole and Jack McCoy's next film *Storm Riders*. Their film of 1982 took the conventional approach to movie making, tripping around the globe capturing the big surf of Hawaii, the steamy tropical waves of Indonesia and a bit of the current contest scene as well as capturing the best sailboard riding going down. Hoole and McCoy threw in a handful of interviews and an exploration of the waves of Western Australia. Hmm, or was it South Australia? The film makers were careful not to offend the locals at the deserted, uncrowded and unexploited breaks they captured on film. The best spots were left un-named.

Storm Riders also broke new ground and surprised audiences when it featured the reclusive Wayne Lynch's debut appearance in his first, and last, comedy sequence. The film was also accompanied by a soundtrack from the best local musos of the day, featuring (among others) Mondo Rock, The Models, The Church and Split Enz. And to close the film, Hoole and McCoy may have taken a leaf out of Paul Witzig's movie handbook.

Like Witzig's flick *Evolution*, in its finale *Storm Riders* featured Wayne Lynch surfing overhead backlit lefts somewhere out in the desert. Where Witzig had chosen the dramatic *Bolero* to close *Evolution*, Hoole and McCoy went for something contemporary, using Little River Band's anthemic 'Cool Change', and then, in a charming touch, Dick Hoole listed his parents in the credits. *Storm Riders*, made on a budget of $250,000, went on to gross nearly one million smackers in its first year of release, but the net return for four years of work was not enough to convince either of the two young cinematographers that it was worth having another crack at.

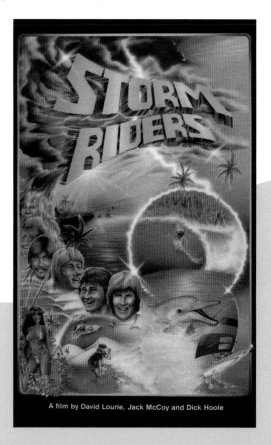

A film by David Lourie, Jack McCoy and Dick Hoole

development of the relatively inexpensive sailboard. These clunky, moulded plastic surfboards with a mast and sail attached became popular first in Europe and then on wave-less lakes and bays along our coastline, then gradually evolved into short manoeuvrable boards that performed in the surf. They could punch through big surf, quickly jibe and ride back along the wave face, and were at their most spectacular taking to the air, as the rider, using the wave as a launching pad, skyrocketed then used the sail to glide (hopefully) back to the water. Wave-jumper boards, better suited to the surf than the smooth-water loving sailboards, had disadvantages: they took time to rig and the small wave-jumpers could be tricky to launch from a 'water start'.

Many surfers who made the transition from surfing to windsurfing found that the required harness caused painful stress in their lower back, and even the most experienced sail-boarders were sometimes caught out by the vagaries of late-afternoon wind shifts, spending the hours before dusk pad-dling an unrigged board back to the beach across a glassy sea.

Meanwhile, some surfers still struggling to paddle their sub-merging shortboards, gave up in frustration and traded in their boards for a new version of the plywood surf ski. The new surf skis, made from injection-moulded plastic, provid-ed an opportunity for big blokes and ex-surfers to get back into the water. Queensland board builder Hayden Kenny and Victorian Fred Pyke had both developed short wave skis made initially from foam and fibreglass, but the modern ver-sion was popularised by Queenscliff lifeguard Michael Petrie and Englishman Roger Shackleton. Their shorter models, fitted with fins and a quick-release seat-belt, could perform like a normal shortboard. They could sprint clear of clean-up sets, Eskimo roll under heavy whitewater, and easily catch waves from well outside the break zone, but unfortunately for other surfers in the water, the ski riders could catch lots of waves in a very short time and on already crowded beaches this reduced the number of waves available for everyone else; friction in the water increased.

The wave ski became popular on beaches on both sides of the continent, but the surf lifesaving fraternity on Gold Coast and Sydney beaches loved them and they became increasingly common in these areas. Petrie took out the first Australian Wave Ski title in 1980, the junior title being won by Hayden Kenny's son Grant who also won Junior and Senior Iron Man titles, both on the same day.

By the mid-1980s, wave-ski riders were common in the line-up of the large sucky waves of Dee-Why Point and Fairy Bower and their cork-like buoyancy often caused

The biggest breakthrough for wind-swept afternoons was the development of the relatively inexpensive sailboard.

⍓ Windsurfers regularly got air long before skateboarders and shortboarders.

⊤ The wave ski was a favourite with older surfers and lifesavers in the late 1980s.

their riders problems. Board riders howled with delight whenever a ski rider took off late and went over the falls, washing in through the soup upside-down, desperately trying to roll their ski upright or at least grab a breath before the ski flipped back into the whitewater. The board surfers quickly dubbed these new wave skis 'goat boats'.

Thrusters and the last remaining twin fins continued to spark the imagination of the next generation of young kids who had rejected the conservative vibe of the previous decade. Bright checks and fluoros dominated clothing as new-wave and power-pop music began to work its way to the surface of beach culture. New fashion palettes had even made their way to wetsuits. Bright wetsuits had already appeared in the 1970s, but were usually only worn by pro surfers in contests or advertising campaigns. Hawaiian Larry Bertleman even appeared at Bells in a wettie with flared legs!

Although the flare concealed a watertight inner cuff it didn't take off. Neither did coloured wetsuits which, in the 1970s, somehow suggested (for men at least) that your

> **Board riders howled with delight whenever a ski rider took off late and went over the falls, washing in through the soup upside-down, desperately trying to roll their ski upright or at least grab a breath before the ski flipped back into the whitewater.**

sexual orientation wasn't quite right or that you were a bit of a two-bob lair. Of course, any surfer will tell you that surfers aren't conservative, they just don't like lairs who dress differently, especially in the water. But fashions change and so does technology, and by the mid 1980s, Piping Hot, Rip Curl and O'Neill were all offering wetsuits in bright smoothy rubber.

The next wave of young Australian surfers were quickly progressing through the maze of professional contests sprouting across the country. These events were sponsored by everything from major surf companies, multinational firms (Pepsi, BHP and Philishave) and emerging surf companies (Mango, Hot Tuna and 100% Mambo) to small local companies. One Woolongong event was sponsored by Mr Juicy!

The youngest surfers, originally called gremlins, but now known as grommets, grommies, or simply groms, got their big chance with the Pro Junior, held on Sydney's northern beaches. The Pro Junior event unearthed a wealth of talent, including Joe Engel, Mark Occhilupo and a chunky Sunshine Coast surfer with the nickname 'Kong'.

Gary 'Kong' Elkerton first appeared as a blond brute in the mould of Ian Cairns and Simon Anderson, sharing their ability to push surfing to the edge while still exhibiting a depth of style and panache. Kong could rip up the small surf with the best of them, but the true scope of his surfing wasn't revealed until the waves got big and juicy. His profile got a big push when he featured in the Quiksilver promotional short Kong's Island. A low-brow adolescent surfing fantasy, it also featured Rabbit Bartholomew and James Jennings. It screened as a special feature with Storm Riders and then appeared as a short with another Quiksilver sponsored feature, the surf video The Performers. Although Elkerton still came across as a big kid, his surfing in the large Hawaiian surf showed he had a future as a professional surfer.

⏏ On land grommets always stick together, partly to keep away from packs of vengeful older surfers who haven't forgiven their indiscretions in the water.

Surfing on the Box

While *The Performers* marked the debut of the surfing video as a promotional tool, the claim for the production of the first Australian surfing video belonged to Victorian ex-surf movie distributor, Colin Turner, and his video *All Time Bells*, which captured the giant surf of Easter 1981. It was another four years before a surf company would attempt to cash in on the immediacy of video production technology. In 1987, Billabong released their first promotional surfvid, *Surf into Summer*, and since then surf companies have regularly churned out a stream of quick-grab features highlighting their endorsed riders parading the latest season's surfwear range.

Gary 'Kong' Elkerton first appeared as a blond brute in the mould of Ian Cairns and Simon Anderson, sharing their ability to push surfing to the edge while still exhibiting a depth of style and panache.

➔ Gary 'Kong' Elkerton at Burleigh Heads. 'Kong' carried on the power turn tradition of Nat and Ian Cairns, but went more vertical.

Kong took his small wave surfing technique to Hawaii and stunned onlookers with his approach to the big North Shore surf. Where most surfers carved off the bottom and slashed back just under the lip, Elkerton, just as he did in the smaller tubes of the Sunshine Coast, blasted onto the top of the lip and rode the crashing curtain back to the bottom. Sure there was not a lot of finesse, that came later, but he showed that when the waves had push, he was happy to push back just as hard.

⊤ Rip Curl went 'pop' when they were joined by Australian Crawl as co-sponsors of the Easter Pro at Bells in 1985.

The Sound of Retro Surf
Even though the swinging sounds of surf music had long gone down the gurgler, pop music still resonated with its influence. Crowds who stumbled into small Sydney bars and pubs to catch a little-known local band, Ebb Tide and the Shore breakers, were amazed to discover it was Midnight Oil doing unannounced gigs!

Girl ripper Pam Burridge got together with Celibate Rifles' personality spunk Damien Lovelock to form the shortlived Pam and the Passions at the same time as another retro-pop and surf band appeared on the Sydney scene. Known as Midget and the Farrellys, and later Midget and the Mod Cons, they were a side project for Dave Faulkner, a Perth guitarist who had relocated to Sydney and ended up as head honcho of cult twangers, the Hoodoo Gurus.

The Hoodoo Gurus revisited 60s power-pop and built up a large following on campuses across the United States, and in Australia courtesy of MTV coverage of their single 'What's My Scene?' They followed it with 'Like Wow Wipeout!' and 'Leilani' with its mondo chants of 'ooomgawa, ooomgawa'. Both tracks sounded like they were written for the score of a *Gilligan's Island* episode. But it was Melbourne popsters Australian Crawl who decided to show solidarity with the growing surf industry when, in 1985, they joined with Rip Curl and co-sponsored the Easter Classic. Aussie Crawl didn't perform at the event, but their latest album sure got a lot of airplay over the contest PA system. Mental as Anything joined the fray with 'Surf and Mull and Sex and Fun' and ...

...100% Mambo had a view to the future while looking the past squarely in the eye when, in the mid and late 1980s, they revisited the Battle of the Surf Bands, a concept popular in early 60s California surf culture. Held in clubs around inner-city Sydney, the battles were hosted by a Mr H.G. Nelson and judged by music luminaries such as Toby Cresswell, editor of *Rolling Stone*. True surf bands were rare at these events, most of which were contested by well-known bands playing under an alias. It must be said that rehearsal time must have been limited for some of the competitors.

On the other hand, a slick and polished Midnight Oil had become *the* musical surf conscience by the mid-1980s. Their increasingly strident lyrics and gnashing guitars reflected a growing anger that many young beachgoers had with the gradual deterioration of water quality.

Joining Elkerton in his journey up the ratings ladder were Barton Lynch, Damian Hardman, Rob Bain and Nicky Wood. Although Newport's Tom Carroll had spent 1983 and 84 as world champion, another Tom, Californian Tom Curren, had grabbed the reins for the next two seasons and would go on to dominate competitive surfing for the next decade.

Curren was a shot in the arm for Californian surfing and was the first American surfer since David Nuuhiwa who was capable of ending the dominance of surfers from the southern hemisphere (South African champion Shaun

Midnight Oil's increasingly strident lyrics and gnashing guitars reflected a growing anger that many young beachgoers had with the gradual deterioration of water quality.

Thomson had claimed the title in 1977 and was the only non-Aussie to take a title until Curren.) and he had the pedigree to back up his list of junior successes, including an amateur World Junior Championship in 1980 on (gasp!) Australia's Gold Coast.

Tom's father, Pat, was a respected big-wave surfer from the era when big waves were a real big deal. His gut-wrenching drops in giant surf at Waimea Bay and Makaha made him a legend of big-wave surfing, and although his balsa gun boards were prized for their beautiful sleek lines and quality craftsmanship, Pat shunned the praises and remained a reluctant hero.

Australian surfers continued to make Hawaii their big-wave Mecca, but as surfers continued to explore our wilder coastlines, some remarkable big wave discoveries were found in our

own backyard. West of Victoria's Cape Otway, where the coast faces directly into the swell generated by the Roaring Forties, big-wave surfers found the Australian mainland's biggest mongrel of a wave. This giant peeling right-hander, breaking along a line of cliffs, was commonly known as Two Mile Bay, but contemporary magazines dubbed it Easter Reef and surfers visiting Victoria for the Rip Curl Easter event made it a 'must surf' destination whenever it looked like breaking. It was first surfed in the early 1960s by Brian Lowden and Bryan Poynton, two surfers from the Ocean Road hamlet of Wye River.

Although Two Mile Bay is not a consistent surf destination, touring pro Tom Curren found the wave to his liking and made regular trips 'down south' to surf there. Tom shared his father's taciturn demeanor, but his surfing was flash and flamboyant. Rip Curl had quickly snaffled him up with a sponsorship deal that made him a wealthy young man even though he was uncomfortable in the glare of the limelight.

Two Mile's reputation as the country's largest rideable wave was not challenged until the late 1990s when Tasmanian surfers spread the word about their latest discovery, an isolated big wave spot they named Shipstern.

Although Australian Tom Carroll had taken out the Pro World Title in 1984, he had other things on his mind when, in 1985, the tour swung towards South Africa. Carroll put his conscience and the welfare of other people first when he boycotted the South African leg of the world tour because of his opposition to the apartheid policies of the

⮕ Torquay's Jeff Sweeney gun-running at
Two Mile Bay on Victoria's far west coast.

⊕ Californian Tom Curren won the Rip Curl Pro in 1985 after an epic semi-final against Mark Occhilupo.

⊕ A young Tom Carroll proudly displays his sponsors' logos, a year before signing a lucrative deal with Quiksilver.

'**Things** have been going **well** for me.'
Tom Carroll, 1987

South African Government. His stance caused a bit of a stir, not just on the pro circuit and in the pages of the surf press. Tom also attracted favourable mainstream press support and earned the admiration of populist Prime Minister Bob Hawke, quickly becoming a darling of the media. At the time, Tom was sponsored by Instinct, a surf-wear company operated by ex-South African professional surfer Mike Tomson, cousin of 1977 world champ Shaun Tomson. When his contract with Instinct ended shortly afterwards, he was soon back among the big bickies when he signed with Quiksilver.

By the mid-1980s, each major surf-wear company had groomed a stable of hotties and Billabong had signed a Cronulla goofy-foot with a mouthful-of-marbles surname, Mark Occhilupo. 'Occy' possessed a prodigious surfing talent and combined it with a singular lack of tact. At a time when sponsored surfers were under increasing pressure to 'act professionally', Occy just couldn't keep his mouth under control. Like all good Aussie teen rippers, he blitzed in the pro events, then bagged the visiting American pros in the surf media. And in doing so, endeared himself to every blond goofy-footer up and down the coast.

Like all good Aussie teen rippers, Occy blitzed in the pro events, then bagged the visiting American pros in the surf media. And in doing so, endeared himself to every blond goofy-footer up and down the coast.

The dollar-driven, high-powered surf comps, and the press pack that followed, propelled contest surfing towards mainstream sport, full of gossip, hyperbole and superlatives. Sections of the surf media lapped it up and for a while it was painted as Us versus Them … Curren versus Carroll, then Curren versus Occhilupo.

In the early 1960s, the show-stopping surfing move was the nose-ride, then the re-entry, and by the late 60s, full-wrap cutbacks. In the early 70s, deep tube riding took centre stage, followed by the snapback of the early 80s, but a surfer from the central coast of New South Wales can claim credit for the eighties move, the floater.

Once Sanga proved it could be done, the floater became a potent weapon in every contest surfer's repertoire.

Mark 'Sanga' Sainsbury, a spiky-haired talent from Avoca, may not have been the first kid to float over sections. After all, it wasn't the 'floating over' that was the problem; it was landing at the bottom without breaking your board, or leg – but there seems little doubt that Sanga was the first to land the floater consistently, stunning judges at the 1984 New South Wales State titles when he first unveiled the new move. Once he proved it could be done, the floater became a potent weapon in every contest surfer's repertoire. Sanga went on to win the 1985 Pro Junior, the 1986 National Amateur titles and a string of other victories. But in 1992 he was found floating in the surf, five hundred metres off Avoca Beach. He had apparently suffered a cerebral haemorrhage as he walked across rocks to surf his local break. He died two months short of his twenty-sixth birthday.

Sanga had grown up surfing the beautiful beaches and quiet coves of the New South Wales Central coast that were yet to be despoiled by pollution and the trappings of encroaching suburbia but by 1983, the situation only 50 kilometres south, on Sydney's suburban beaches, had become so bad that the authorities were forced to lengthen the waste disposal pipes and erect warning signs advising swimmers of the poor water quality. Surfers at Victoria's Thirteenth Beach and Gunnamatta experience the same problems. Some Sydney beaches were closed until prevailing wind and surf conditions washed away the filth. But the solution smacked of an 'out of sight, out of mind' mentality – the same volume of waste still entered the waters off Sydney heads, it just entered the water further out.

A Cold War that was continuing to raise the spectre of nuclear destruction also haunted surfers across the nation and board riders voiced their concerns at a series of semi-pro events on the Gold Coast known as the SAND contests. Surfers against Nuclear Destruction was set up by local board riders Dennis Callinan, Rabbit Bartholomew and ex-Sydney southsider Geoff Doig. With the help of Midnight Oil and Spy V Spy, the events attracted everyday Gold Coast rippers as well as the cream of the world's surfers, with representatives from up to sixteen different nations. Cheyne Horan and Pam Burridge won the inaugural events of 1985, and when the event was conducted once more in 1987, the winners were Chappy Jennings and Wendy Botha. The SAND events certainly grabbed the headlines and were the subject of a television documentary that received an International Peace Media Award.

Surfers at Kirra, mindful of the effects of building the groyne there in the early 1970s, were constantly battling 'the authorities' who, under pressure from boat-loving entrepreneurs, decided that what the Gold Coast really needed was a marina. A couple of seawalls at Kirra Point was all that was needed, the entrepreneurs said. Just add some retail outlets and a vast car park and everyone would benefit. Who would really miss a world-class surf spot? they asked. The Gold Coast was already in the midst of a building boom: vacant blocks of beach-side sand were sprouting multi-storeyed apartments that towered into the sky, reducing Australia's growing skin cancer epidemic by shading acres of sand every afternoon.

However, through the efforts of local councillors who actually surfed and a committed bunch of locals who formed KEPT (Kirra Environmental Protection Trust), the proposed Kirra Marina was defeated – for the time being at least.

If there was big money in pleasure boats, there was increasingly more money in surfing, but small local surf shops, usually run by crusty local shapers who whipped up boards for the locals and contented themselves with a couple of racks of T-shirts, boardies and wetties, were under increasing pressure to keep up with the surf mega-stores with their stands of computer-shaped Thrusters. The Thruster had become the most popular shape

⊤ South African pro surfer Shaun Thomson shares the limelight with the 'Cheetah' bikini girls.

⊤ Pro surfers are a well-dressed, fun-loving bunch of guys. Left to right: Tom Curren, Willy Morris, Glenn Winton, Mark Price, Barton Lynch, Tom Carroll, Wes Laine, Martin Potter, Nicky Wood, Terry Richardson.

⊟ Pam Burridge was one of the first Aussie girls to throw a big fan of spray.

⊤ Tucked up in a tight tube looking for a way out.

for standard shortboards; indeed, it had become the only shape. So with board design stagnating, or at least remaining conservative, shaping machines appeared.

Large surf companies, cashed up by the 80s boom, began using basic computer software hooked up to a machine that shaved a blank down to its required dimensions, leaving the shaper with only a few minor adjustments to deal with, like fine sanding, or adding their signature to finished blanks before the board was ready for glassing.

> The Thruster had become the most popular shape for standard shortboards; indeed, it had become the only shape. So with board design stagnating, or at least remaining conservative, shaping machines appeared.

The surf industry flourished (fuelled partly by a sudden infatuation across the United States with surfing and Australian surf wear) and more and more surf shops opened up, ready to exploit the growing market. Paul and Rick Neilson, who had started their first small retail outlet in Surfers Paradise, now operated a string of surf shops up and down the coast, all chock-a-block with products from 'the big three' (Ripcurl, Quiksilver and Billabong), and other chain stores staffed by quasi surf-dudes were cashing in on the boom.

The world of retail chains, sponsorship signings, bid, counter-bid and celebrity status was not without its pitfalls and some of Australia's most talented young surfers wilted under the pressure, either blowing their chances by spending more time on the party circuit than in the water, or simply preferring to surf with their mates away from the scrutiny of the surf media.

Joe Engel, Jason Buttenshaw, Gary Green and Nicky Wood, all talented contest surfers, eventually bailed from the contest circuit with their competitive potential unfulfilled. In 1987 Wood, at the age of sixteen, had been the youngest winner of the Rip Curl Pro. Mark Occhilupo, whose wild, free surfing had made him a darling of the surf press and every other young goofy-foot in the country, had also lost his appetite for competition. His 'head-to-head' semi final with Tom Curren in the 1986 Bells Pro set a new benchmark for competitive surfing. Like two heavyweight prize fighters, both surfers had slugged it out in overhead waves,

⬆ Gary Green from Cronulla styles underneath a thick lip. Green was another great Aussie surfer who chose to go surfing with his mates, rather than follow the gruelling Pro Tour.

Some of Australia's most talented young surfers wilted under the pressure, either blowing their chances by spending more time on the party circuit than in the water, or simply preferring to surf with their mates away from the scrutiny of the surf media.

each pushing the other into wild floaters and hair-raising bottom turns. Curren had gone on to win the event, but all Occy had to do was to remain focused and surely a future world title crown would be his.

He finished ninth on the world ratings in 1987, then lost interest, and was left to struggle with his own inner demons. It took him ten years to fight his way through the grind of the circuit; chasing the tails of a fresh batch of Californian and Aussie hot-rats before he could regain his place in pro surfing's top ten.

While Occy's competitive world collapsed around him, Gary 'Kong' Elkerton decided it was time to put his head down and bum up and get serious about his pro career. Like Occhilupo, Kong's reputation was built around explosive free surfing which had spectators and potential sponsors frothing at the mouth. So in January of 1988, Gary sent off a handwritten letter to all the surfing press, telling them he no longer wished to be referred to as the lip-bashing giant, 'Kong'; he was now simply Gary Elkerton, professional surfer.

A lucrative contract with Californian surf-wear company Ocean Pacific followed, but when the juicy waves of the Hawaiian winter were reduced to a minor role on the circuit, Elkerton faced a future of contests decided in mush-burger beach breaks. He would never take out the title, finishing runner-up in 1987, 1990 and 1993.

Barton Lynch, Damien Hardman, Carroll and Elkerton had been joined at the top of the ratings ladder by three new goofy-footers – Rob Bain, Glen Winton and Dave McCaulay – and natural footer Bryce Ellis, and while they were making a comfortable living from tour results and endorsements, the most lucrative sponsorship deal of all went to Tom Carroll, who negotiated a million-dollar contract with Torquay surf company Quiksilver.

Pam Burridge now had a handful of young protegés snapping at her leg-rope. From Western Australia came Jodie Cooper, who had grown up pushing through the heaving WA shore breaks and paddling over the edge of monster lips along Margaret River's coast. There was Pauline Menczer from Sydney, who saved her bickies, fought off a debilitating arthritic condition and, through a simple combination of g&d and skill, battled her way into the top eight in 1988. She was joined not long after by Toni Sawyer and Michelle Donoghoe but most of the girls on the circuit had to make do with smaller contest purses and fewer sponsorship opportunities.

Skateboards reappeared in the latter half of the decade, as surfing started to cross over to street-savvy 'attitood' and fashion. The new skateboards, with their wide kick-tail decks, precision bearings and graffiti-art inspired graphix, grabbed the attention of a new generation of teenagers who were increasingly disaffected by a bland youth culture offering them stadium rock, distressed denim and nothing else. These pre gen-X teenagers took their new boards and ollied them around city streets looking for smooth drainage channels or slabs of slick concrete.

What's that Rash? On the beach fashion scene, the wonder fabric Lycra, a body-clinging material that allowed high-waisted bikinis to be tugged up to the wearer's armpits and helped create the miniscule 'tanga' bikini, was also appearing on men's racks as a new piece of surf apparel, the rash vest. Almost overnight, sand-encrusted jars of Vaseline, the surfer's friend, disappeared from glove boxes and wetsuit bins across the country. Surfboard wax suffered the same fate and, for the next five surf seasons, the petrified, yellowing lumps of honey wax were discarded as most surfers switched to Gorilla Grip, a sheet of thin, rough, rubbery foam glued to a board's deck to aid grip.

When there was none to be found, they turned their attention to building their own ramps and half-pipes, and as ramp after ramp grew bigger some reached lengths of thirty feet with ends fifteen feet high. These giant half-pipes became the big waves of skating, and touring pro skaters journeyed to Australia for the first of the sponsored 'Ramp Riots' which often ran in tandem with pro surfing contests. Surf companies quickly capitalised on the new skate boom and increasingly their clothing ranges included longer and longer, sweat-inducing baggy pants and shorts.

Californian surfer–skaters Tony Hawke and Christian Fletcher found that, whereas for years skating had copied surf moves, new concave decks and tiny wheels enabled them to translate their skate moves into surfing. New-skool skate moves such as 'shove-its', 'stale-fish', 'airgrabs' and 'lip tricks' crossed over to the surf lexicon.

The most lucrative sponsorship deal of all went to Tom Carroll, who negotiated a million-dollar contract with Torquay surf company Quiksilver.

⬆ Tom Carroll's low centre of gravity and stocky build helps him bank along the lip while maintaining maximum revs.

⊕ Pauline Menczer grimaces as she bounces the foam.

Board riders rated the bodyboarders slightly ahead of goat boat riders and religious extremists but slightly behind the increasing number of longboard riders. They dubbed bodyboarders 'Esky-lid riders', 'sponge riders' or 'speed humps'!

Meanwhile beachgoers were increasingly finding Tom Morey's Boogie to be the perfect surf craft. It was light, relatively cheap, relatively painless if you were sconned by one and relatively indestructible unless your Alsatian pup took a liking to it and was far more comfortable than the nipple-destroing Coolite kick board. And Boogies were fun and took no skill whatsoever to use. No need to worry about getting to your feet … just find a wave, point towards the shore and kick.

Not disadvantaged by the split-second commitment needed by stand-up board riders to get to their feet, some Boogie riders found that they could launch their spongey vehicles into horrendous waves. Hairball spots like Cronulla's Shark Island and Western Australia's The Box were suddenly filled with crazed bodyboarders kicking frantically into shallow-bottomed, ledgy barrels and popping out the other end. Mike Stewart, world bodyboarding champ eight times over, kick-started the aggressive 'go for it' mindset of kids in Oz when he won the Morey Boogie Pro-Am at Cronulla Point in eight- to ten-foot surf.

But board riders weren't impressed. Bodyboards could be spun around within their own length in the take-off zone. Surfers paddling into backwash-ripped take-offs would suddenly find that the small Pinke Zinke 'n' Clearasil-coated kid drifting beside them had spun in a flash, taken the inside position, kicked into the wave, sprayed the board rider with saltwater and abuse and, without the need to spring to their feet, disappeared into the tube.

Board riders rated the bodyboarders slightly ahead of goat boat riders and religious extremists but slightly behind the increasing number of longboard riders. They dubbed bodyboarders 'Esky-lid riders', 'sponge riders' or 'speed humps'!

After a decade of verbal abuse, some wave-ski riders finally saw the error of their ways and went back to the board that got them surfing in the first place: the Malibu. Other aging surfers, now free of family responsibilities, scrounged around under their holiday shacks and came up with yellowing longboards that hadn't seen saltwater for decades. Others, more cashed up, ordered lightweight replicas of the boards they had grown up riding.

Wafer-thin Thrusters and miniscule twin fins always struggle to stay afloat in smaller than knee-high surf and since the late 1960s the picture-perfect tiny surf of summer beach breaks such as The Pass and Currumbin Alley, and of southern reefs like The Trough near Adelaide or Point Impossible or The Pines in Victoria, had gone unridden – until longboarders rediscovered them.

The gliding style of longboarding breathed fresh air into the lungs of older surfers and their kids (especially their daughters), and a small, vibrant longboard circuit sprang into being. In 1986, while Tom Curren and South African Wendy Botha were taking out the world championships on the shortboard pro tour, Nat

⬆ Skateboard moves rapidly translated to surfing, and vice versa, but the skate terminology had a lot of older surfers scratching their heads. This is a 'frontside air'.

⬇ It's been said that in every Australian household there is a Seekers album, and at least one bodyboard. Alas, I have no Seekers album and someone must have two bodyboards!

↑ Nat Young and Californian Joel Tudor cross tracks on their modern longboards.

← Looking in your surf dictionary for the definition of the term 'S' turn? Andrew Egan comes up with the perfect example.

Young came out of retirement, took a break from his modelling career, dusted off his longboard and took the first world longboard title.

Back in the shortboard world, Californian Tom Curren claimed the 1985 and 86 world championships and would return to regain his title in 1990, but two Australian goofy-footers, Damien Hardman and Barton Lynch, kept Aussie pro surfing in the limelight. Hardman, from the heavy water of North Narrabeen, took the title in 1987. At first he appeared to be just another small wave ripper, but he wasn't. Hardman's surfing was polished and precise, in big surf and small, and it was his ability to squeeze more turns out of every wave that took him to the top of the pro surfing ratings again in 1991.

Barton Lynch, a savvy competitor from North Steyne, followed Hardman's victory with a triumph of his own the following year. Like Hardman, Lynch had been unjustly tagged as a small-wave specialist, but in the Billabong Pro of 1988, held in thick and beautiful twelve-foot surf at the Banzai Pipeline, Barton slotted himself into enough tubes to take out the event, knocking off the hottest hometown surfers in the process.

Lynch's eloquent and easygoing nature made him good copy. He was a regular in surfing and mainstream media, but he raised eyebrows when, at the peak of his career, he claimed in an interview that, to some people, tennis was just as much fun as surfing. A quick read of his quote and, sure, he did seem just like any other mercenary soulless ocker. But those who read his quote carefully had to agree: to some surfing is just fun and nothing more. The fact that Lynch was having fun and earning a lot of money doing it raised the hackles of many of the 'groovier than thou' soul surfers.

The conquests of our surfing professionals were being documented in an ever-growing number of surf magazines and videos. From 1985 through to the end of 1990, only three Australian surf movies were released – Grant Young's corny *Mad Wax*, Ronnie Gorringe's *Indo Express* and Paul Witzig's *All Down the Line*. *All Down the Line* highlighted surfers on the Quiksilver team, and included a fine soundtrack featuring the works of The Black Sorrows, Big Pig, Noiseworks and Dennis Nattras. All three films did brief business on the shrinking surf-movie circuit then were quickly released on video. In the same period, twenty-one 'video only' surf flicks were released!

The celluloid features that documented surfing's rough-edged history took a back seat as the dumbed-down immediacy of video splashed the latest contest footage across television screens within weeks of the action taking place. Now, the action can be played over and over again, paused, rewound and studied frame by frame. No longer do lines of surfers queue up outside local halls, pay their money and file in to watch brilliant flickering tubes on larger-than-life screens, accompanied by the rattle and hum of a wheezy Hanimex projector. No longer do surfers have to con their girl into a night watching surf movies at the local surf club. Now their line is 'Do ya wanna watch a video? Umm, I mean a surf video!'

'I saw this **fly** against the wall, **darting** back and forth, and you **should** be able to do that on a wave.'
Cheyne Horan, 1982

⊕ Cheyne Horan floats above the fluid.

'There's times I **sit out** there and it's so crowded ...
I hate the fact that it is becoming ridiculously
popular. It's a huge dilemma. I've got to make a
living. What am I going to do? **Give up** and go work
in a Seven/Eleven.'
Barton Lynch, 1991

⊤ Manicured lawns out the front, with the
manicured lines of Lennox Head in the
distance.

⊕ The surf at North Narrabeen has been
responsible for churning out top-notch
surfers for decades. Local goofy-footer
Damian Hardman, shown here surfing
a left much like The Alley at North Narra,
went on to be world Champion in 1987
and again in 1991.

→ It's simple really ... the more speed —
the further you float. Luke Egan goes for
distance and floats along the blur at
Kirra Point.

Surfing Goes to the Extreme

The retail surfing boom of the 1980s was at its most dynamic in the landlocked cities of the American mid-west and Aussie surf wear and pro surfers became the flavour of the month along the coastal strands of California and Florida. Over an eighteen-month period, Californian magazines *Surfer* and *Surfing* almost doubled in thickness as new surf companies clambered to buy advertising space.

Then in a flash, it was all gone – fluoros, slash artwork, tight shorts all dumped into the clearance bins of active-wear shops across the States. The fad and fashion of 80s surfing flickered and went out and many shooting-star labels went with them.

At home, we were rocked by the 1987 recession that had banks and building societies reeling; and many small surf companies, undercapitalised and overcommitted, went to the wall. Only the major surf companies hung on – some of them by the skin of their teeth. The repercussions of the collapse of 87 lasted well into the 1990s, rejigging our concept of leisure time. Flexi-time, RDOs, nine-day fortnights and part-time jobs all continued to change the amount of time we spent at the beach.

For most of us, the long summer break or annual leave holidays had been the best time to set out looking for waves, but our leisure time became more precious. If you wanted to get good waves on your holidays, you had to maximise your chances by heading for a destination where good surf was guaranteed. Which, for most surfers, meant hitting Queensland in cyclone season or Hawaii in the northern-hemisphere winter. While the chance of catching premium surf at these destinations is good, the chance of finding these destinations without crowds is not so good. But there are places where the surf is remarkably consistent and crowds minimal. And if you want to play, you have to pay.

The late 1980s and early 90s saw the appearance of surf camps: resorts with exclusive rights to a patch of reef, a strip of coast or even a whole island. Surf camps are

destinations that cater for surfers who have saved up their hard-earned bickies and aren't prepared to waste them on two weeks of crowded junk surf. Although there are no surf camps per se along the Australian coast, there are a handful of tour operators who can strap you into a four-wheel drive, treat you to an Aussie-style surf experience, and drop you back at your apartment before the salt water dries off your back.

Other surfers have chosen Indonesia, sampling the surf camps of Sumbawa or the Javanese jungle resort-camp of Grajagan, where one of the planet's best left-handers peels down a coral reef; a camp where tigers prowl the jungles of the national park behind the beach and where a recent tidal wave surged ashore one night, destroyed the camp and washed a handful of pro surfers through the jungle for a couple of hundred metres. Some have searched further along the Indonesian archipelago to the Mentawais, a small group of islands dotted with fantastic lefts and rights. There's no surf camp on these islands but boats ranging from luxury cruisers to leaky timber vessels prowl these waters. Sadly, even in this remote untouched slice of the planet, the waters of the Mentawais are soiled – choked with the trash and twenty-first century detritus that washes ashore … and not from the tour boats, but from polluted cities thousands of

miles away. Each season, surfers spend upwards of A$250 per day to sample these glorious waves.

Other surfers have chosen a getaway in Fiji. Tavarua, a footy-ground-sized tropical island, is home to another near-perfect left, just off the sand, called Restaurants. The American lessees of the island have sole rights to the waves of Restaurants and only paying guests of the island may surf there. Unfortunately, for the guests, Restaurants is less consistent than one particular break not under the control of the lessees. Reachable only by boat, this is Cloudbreak, another world-class left-hander.

In the Indian Ocean are the Maldives, a nation of atolls that lie like foliage-stained teardrops shed upon a tropic ocean. In a story straight out of *Robinson Crusoe*, the Maldives were discovered (surfwise) in 1973 when two Australian surfers, Tony Hinde and Mark Scanlon, crew members on a ketch bound for Africa, were stranded on an outer atoll after their vessel had run aground in the inky blackness of an Indian Ocean night. They survived the wreck and in the weeks that followed, while salvage operations were underway, discovered atoll after atoll with great waves peeling along rubbly coral shores. The surfers kept their discovery secret for nearly a decade, but word gradually spread about this new destination. Hinde eventually made the Maldives his home, converted to Islam, married, and began to open up his discovery to the rest of the surfing world.

⊕ Initially, skateboarding was just a way of going downhill while pretending you were surfing, but now it's considered to be an extreme sport, and here's why.

When the next wave of skateboarding arrived and united with grunge, youth culture had a new pulse that rapidly beat its way to surf culture.

Surf camps are not, however, the reason to visit Puget Sound, a strip of cold fog-racked coast in the northwest corner of continental USA. Instead, it boasts a vibrant nightlife scene that is as far removed from surf culture as is possible to imagine and in the early 1990s a group of young musicians created a sound there that swept across youth culture as quickly as surf music had done thirty years previously.

The new sound borrowed from 60s fuzz guitar, echo and feedback, dispensed with 60s pop lightness and replaced it with angst and narcotic-fuelled despair. The music also borrowed from 70s punk and no-wave styles and was bleak, introspective and catchy. Labelled 'grunge', it shot to prominence courtesy of Kurt Cobain, his band Nirvana, and other outfits like Pearl Jam and Bad Religion. The grunge 'non-style' summed up how a lot of kids were feeling about the world: alienated!

In response to the big-shoulder-pad 80s, the preening of punk, the glitter-glam of disco or Carnaby Street flower power, grunge was downbeat. When the next wave of skateboarding arrived and united with grunge, youth culture had a new pulse that rapidly beat its way to surf culture. This non-style was quickly picked up by surf-wear companies who developed whole ranges of monochrome hooded sweats and layered them with check flannelette shirts, baggy trousers, beanies and faux weather-beaten jackets.

It was a big jump for surf culture and it applied not only to the skateboarding crossover. Snowboarding, another variation on the theme of going downhill fast without a motor, also grew in popularity. The single ski, an early version of the snowboard, had been around since Californian surfer and 1964 world title finalist Mike Doyle developed a version in the early 1970s. Doyle's early versions, with their feet-together stance, showed promise but failed simply because they were in the right place but at the wrong time. A later board with a deep swallow and no bindings, the Winterstick, also failed to capture the imagination of the general public. But when someone finally came up with the idea of attaching bindings to snowboards so that your feet were not placed parallel but lined up as you would for surfing or skateboarding, the whole thing fell into place and surfboard riding bio-mechanics crossed effortlessly into snowboarding, spawning another 'extreme' sport.

⊕ Damian Hardman cools off during a press conference.

For two decades, surf wear and beach wear had been summery, utilitarian and unsuccessfully copied by pretend surfers and clothing companies eager to attach their reputations to surfing. But now, the once-unique surf culture was doing the mimicking. Street, grunge and skate styles started to call the shots, and the long skate shorts, which were great for keeping your crotch perspiration-free while skating, were adopted by the surf labels as boardshorts.

Extra long boardies may be great for skating but they aren't so good for surfing – they catch on the knee and tangle between the thighs. Fashion, though, was shaping the look, not practicality, and as the 90s progressed, boardshorts grew longer and longer. But there was, and still is, one practical use for the ever-growing boardie: protecting legs from the sun's rays.

'I started surfing on a **bodyboard**, but I'm glad I got off it when I did. One thing all surfers have to admit though is the alternative **surfcraft** are good for a go from time to time. Bodyboards in shorey close-outs and **mals** when its micro.'
Kelly Slater, 1991

For generations Australians had baked themselves silly under the summer sun, and a golden tan became a badge of honour for surfers and sun seekers the country over. Until some scientists discovered that lots of sun could do other things to you, like cause deadly melanomas and skin cancer. Most beachgoers put this discovery down to more sour grapes from 'the authorities' trying to limit the amount of fun you could have in not much clothing, and when scientists claimed the best way to protect oneself from sunborne illness was covering up, most thought 'Yeah sure! What? And not get a tan? No way!'

So swimmers and surfers ignored the advice and continued to baste themselves in tanning oils and lotions. Some older sunbathers, with skin weathered and tanned like old boots, still used secret blends, passed down from generation to generation, that comprised (in equal parts) flytox, vinegar, camphor oil and kerosene. But scientists at the CSIRO pointed to Australia's growing rate of skin cancer and cited statistics that showed, conclusively, that the citizens of Queensland had the highest rate of skin cancer in the western world.

⊤ Little kids eventually mastered the Surf-O-Plane and used to ride the things standing up. You can stand on a bodyboard, but try doing this on a surfo. Jason Hazel flips his lid.

By the middle of the 1990s, Tom Morey's invention, the bodyboard, was the most popular surf craft in the water.

People really sat up and took notice when, towards the end of the 1980s, it was found that the earth's protective layer of ozone was fractured from overuse of aerosol propellants – and that the fracture was quickly turning into a tear, an invisible hole in the atmosphere directly above the southern hemisphere that allowed the sun's ultra-violet rays, unfettered by the ozone layer, to scorch the Australian coast and country.

The sting and tingle of the first sunburn of summer, followed by peeling, a chocolaty suntan and its attendant praise, became a thing of the past as the 'Slip Slop Slap' campaign heightened public awareness of the problem. The rash vest previously worn under wetties became an effective and fashionable addition to the surfer's wardrobe, and parents quickly slipped their kids into full-length Lycra sunsuits, smothered their faces in sun block and kept their heads protected with caps and hats. Thick black wetsuits, which since the 1960s had been used solely in winter, became popular all year round, especially when manufacturers came up with lightweight suits for summer surfing. Finally, girls' suits were cut for feminine body shapes and lightweight wetsuits with floral graphics and fashionable colour palettes kept girls in the water and out of the sun and protected their tummies from bodyboard rash.

Joining suntan as a thing of the past were surf mats, knee boards, Coolites and Surf-o-Planes. By the middle of the 1990s, Tom Morey's invention, the bodyboard, was the most popular surf craft in the water. Plastics firms perfected cheap and reliable copies of Morey's original design and an entry-level board could be bought for as little

← Bodyboarders at a club contest in South Australia.

⊤ Dean Morrison finds relief from the sun.

as twenty dollars. Hi-tech 'Signature Models', endorsed by top riders such as Mike Stewart and Mike Eppelstun, featured slick bottoms, channels and water-resistant cores. The board and sundry accessories, like wrist cords, flippers and board covers, could set back a serious body-boarder around five hundred dollars.

Although lid riders and everyday beachgoers were everywhere on their new bodyboards, it seemed that not so many teenage bodyboard riders were making the switch to 'stand-up' surf-ing. Whether this had any effect on Australia's dominance of pro surfing is any-one's guess, but one thing is for sure: throughout the 1990s, their weren't as many Aussie pro surfers dominating the ratings. The ratings were almost the exclusive domain of Kelly Slater.

Slater, a native of Florida, was seen as the natural successor to Tom Curren, the world champ of 1985, 1986 and 1990, but Slater took Curren's surfing further into the stratosphere. 'Slats' took out the pro tour title an amazing six times, in 1992 and from 1994 to 1998 inclusive, breaking Mark Richards' record (four consecutive titles, 1979

Tuning In Radio surf reports, which had been common on Aussie radio on weekends since the 1960s, sprang up during the 90s on most coastal radio stations, and major newspaper chains also included detailed surf reports. What the 1990s surf reports did share with their 60s counterparts was their inaccuracy. The surf reporter was committed to an early rise and surf check, followed by a quick call to the station for a 'live cross' from the beach before hitting the water themselves. Yeah, sure. Most reports came from the reporter's bedroom as he made the 'cross' after a quick look out the window and formulated an educated guess about the surf based on reports and predictions from mates at the pub the previous evening.

Few surfers took the reports seriously. After all, up-to-the-minute swell information had become available via fax from the Bureau of Meteorology, and towards the end of the decade surf report sites arrived over the Internet. Real Surf, Coastal Watch and Surfshop.com all provide constant updates about the state of the surf. Some sites provide video-stream coverage of beaches, with a new photo of surf conditions at popular beaches every fifteen seconds. With Internet surf reports, the chances of an uncrowded session, or a quick, uncrowded surf before work, have lessened and there's no longer a need to spend endless hours poring over weather maps or making long-distance phonecalls to mates down the coast, pressing them for info on how big the swell might be getting. Just set your PC to wake you at first light. While you're yawning and scratching, the computer dials up the surf report site. You don't need to lift your head from the pillow as the screen flickers with its crack of dawn vision. If it's cranking, you're straight out of bed. If it's onshore, yawn and catch a few more hours' sleep.

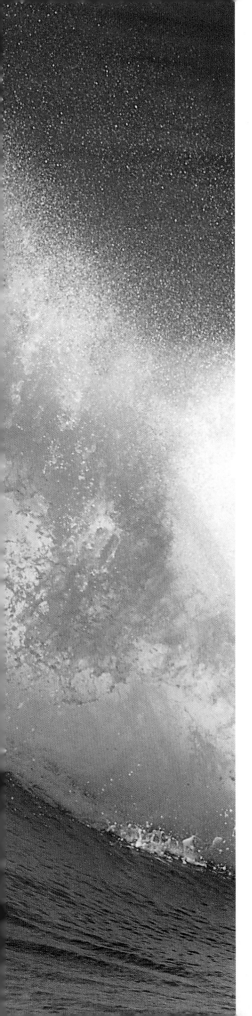

to 1982) in doing so. His dynamic surfing secured him a lucrative contract with Australian surf-wear company Quiksilver, and his bit role in the 1992 series of surf-soapie *Baywatch* didn't hurt his image as a young surfing celebrity face. Nor did his romantic liaison with 1990s blonde-bombshell Pamela Anderson, but there was more to Kelly Slater than just his image.

Slater's surfing was a futuristic blend of rad nu-school moves that crossed over from street skating, and stylish on-edge carves. He could pop airs with the best of them, and could handle the grunt and punch of Hawaii's north shore without batting an eyelid. And in competition he could shut down his rivals with manoeuvres that were almost as radical as his free surfing. Australian hotties struggled to keep up with

> Slater's surfing was a futuristic blend of rad nu-school moves that crossed over from street skating and stylish on-edge carves. He could pop airs with the best of them, and could handle the grunt and punch of Hawaii's north shore without batting an eyelid. And in competition he could shut down his rivals with manoeuvres that were almost as radical as his free surfing.

him and he stitched up Damien Hardman in 1992, Shane Powell in 94, Shane Beschen in 96, Occhilupo in 97 and Michael Campbell in 1998. All great surfers – but in the race to the world title they all came in second best.

Slater's surfing prowess and Quiksilver's marketing machine made Slater a household name and there were circus-like scenes whenever he appeared at a contest. He was continually swamped by giggling girls and pimple-faced grommets looking to grab his autograph or pose beside him for a photo.

Despite Slater's success, Tom Carroll was still seen as the surfer who most epitomised contemporary Aussie surfing, even though his career was drawing to a close.

His competitive zenith had occurred in 1991 when he defeated Hawaiian Derek Ho in the final of the Pipeline Masters winning the event with what may have been the most extraordinary manoeuvre in competitive surfing.

◄ Duranbah Beach. Kelly Slater lays back on the wave and throws a huge curtain of spray. Did he pull it off? Of course – that's why he's won the World Championships a record six times!

In solid ten foot surf at the Banzai Pipeline, Tom, seemingly bluffed into an inside positioning where any take-off, would be suicidal, paddled into a black and glassy Pipeline brute and survived a takeoff so late that he must have been connected to his board by only a toenail embedded in wax. Arriving alive at the base of the wave, he threw a bottom turn that directed him straight back up the wave towards the cascading lip and certain annihilation. But with a snap under the lip, that was as severe as it was precise, redirected his sleek gun board back to the base of the wave, beat the lip to the bottom, squeezed into a small tube, then glided out onto the safety of the shoulder, unscathed and victorious, leaving Ho to wonder why the crowd on the beach at the Pipeline were screaming.

⊕ Kelly Slater edges towards a crowd of fans, all eager for an autograph or a photo opportunity with their hero.

Western Australian Tim Duff, who had been inducted into Surfing Australia's Hall of Fame Honour Roll in 1987 for his team surfing concept, received the honour again in 1992 when he and Jock Campbell introduced the State of Origin surf contests. A team of Aboriginal surfers included in the 1992 event led to the establishment of a series of Koori Surf Contests held initially in the waves of Aussie Pipe at Wreck Bay.

Aussie Pipe, Australia's best east-coast left reef break, has been a popular destination whenever a nor-easter is blowing over a strong groundswell, and 1980 Australian Champion Terry Richardson made his name here with his tube riding and scorching cutbacks through the Aussie Pipe racetrack. Across the bay from the Pipe lies the small Koori community of Wreck Bay, and over the years the country's true locals have made the Pipe their home break.

The success of the Koori team at the State of Origin events led to the formation of a team of surfers and dancers who, with Wayne Lynch as coach and support from Hawaiian surfwear label Da Hui, travelled to Hawaii to compete against native Hawaiians. A further series of Koori contests, sponsored by Billabong and supported by Quiksilver and a host of smaller labels but with no government backing, saw a group of hot indigenous surfers like Ken Dann, Eric Mercy, Andrew Ferguson, Gavin Dickenson and Todd Roberts highlight the growing Koori surf culture. Later events were held along New South Wales' Tweed Coast, but a series of tragic deaths amongst the Koori surfer community sadly saw the events lose momentum.

The Australian pro circuit, with events at Bells, Kirra, Sydney and Margaret River, continued to receive extensive media coverage right through the 1990s. It was a far cry from the virtual media blackout of surfing during the 1960s and early 70s. Pro surfers became regulars on television sports programs, contests were regularly televised, and TV surf programs took regular timeslots on weekend afternoons, especially during summer.

Roy Norris's *Prime Surf TV* became a popular show that continued the tradition of Midget Farrelly's *Surf Show* of 1967 and took out an Australian Surfing Hall of Fame

Award in 1996. Former surf movie makers Jack McCoy and Alby Falzon also catered to the growing surf-on-TV market with their latest offerings. *Bunyip Dreaming* showcased McCoy's cinematic style that was first evident in *Tubular Swells* and *Storm Riders*, and Billabong used his skills to create their promotional videos for the rest of the decade. McCoy's first effort for Billabong, *The Green Iguana*, was quickly followed by *Sons of Fun*, *Sik Joy*, *The Billabong Challenges*, *Alley Oop* and *Wide Open*. Falzon, the creator of *Morning of the Earth*, released *Can't Step Twice on the Same Piece of Water* in 1992 and in 1996 he followed it up with the Quiksilver promotional video *Metaphysical*. Paul Sargeant also released a series of videos, his *Sarge's Surfing Scrapbooks*.

Falzon and McCoy's videos were characterised by their rich colour, vivid lighting and stunning water photography. *Can't Step Twice* was shot on 16 mm then converted to video. It was released to critical acclaim but its slow-paced, dreamlike quality was a strong contrast to the edgy rough-cut style of Californian Taylor Steele's release, *Momentum*. Steele's videos dispensed with the formula successfully marketed by Bruce Brown and copied by Australia's Bob Evans. The accepted formula had been to combine hot action with humour, travel and sunsets. Perhaps Steele had never seen Brown's *The Endless Summer* because, apart from hot action, nothing else resembled the old winning formula.

Momentum contained lots of hectic action as shots jumped from surfer to surfer and beach to beach with no dissolves, no evidence of continuity, and certainly no lingering sunsets. The video appeared to have been assembled from a conglomeration of unedited wild footage and was backed by a soundtrack of jarring, aggressive punk rock. Its raw approach and fast cutting appealed to 90s surfers, possibly because it seemed that anyone with a half-decent video camera could go out and shoot footage of their mates and, without the worry of fancy editing, have the product on the market a couple of weeks later and make themselves rich in the process. It wasn't as simple as it seemed, but Steele's *Momentum* went on to sell nearly fifteen thousand copies in the US alone.

The success of *Momentum* and Steele's follow-ups propelled thrash and punk bands into the surf scene, and when Steele toured Australia with his next feature, *Good Times*, he added to the billing, live performances from Californian rockers Pennywise and Blink-182, and Aussie thrashers Bodyjar. Pennywise became regular visitors to our shores, headlining The Falls festival, which is held over the New Year period on Victoria's west coast. The success of this festival led the promoter, local surfer Simon Daly, to expand his operation and branch out in Torquay to coincide with the Rip Curl Pro at Bells in 1997. Known as the Offshore Festival, it showcases local and international acts and provides camping facilities and buses that zip the festival patrons into Torquay or out to the

'There is a cure for 'the summer-time blues' – it's called **longboarding**. The glide is back to stay.'
Chris Bystrom, 1998

Hollywood Goes Surfing – Again After thirty years of trying, Hollywood still couldn't figure out surfing. In 1991, Keanu Reeves, Patrick Swayze, Lori Petty and Gary Busey starred in the action movie *Point Break*. Local surfing audiences howled with laughter when the film reached its 'thrilling' climax. The *Point Break* action switched to 'the largest surfable waves in the world, dude.' Yes, a surf spot that all well-respected masked bank robbers know as Bells Beach! Surfers could probably forgive Hollywood's indiscriminate use of superlatives, but to show Bells to be just a short walk from a railway station at Torquay (nope, nearest railway line is twenty kilometres away!), to be surrounded by fir trees (nope, just tea tree scrub, not even a spindly blue gum) and then, horror of horrors, the biggest wave in the world as ... a left? Co-star Gary Busey, a part-time surfer himself, should have known better, having starred in John Milius' 70s cult movie *Big Wednesday*. As 'Leroy the Masochist' he'd emulated the deeds and misdeeds of 60s Californian surfers. Somewhere along the way, you'd have thought that Busey might have told *Point Break*'s producers that Bells was a right-hander!

contest site at Bells. For Daly, a little bit of surf savvy went a long way and he went on to receive a Young Australian of the Year Award.

Another American surf movie maker, Chris Bystrom, who had set up home on the Gold Coast, followed in Bob Evans's tradition and released surf movies and videos on almost an annual basis. His first efforts, including *Secret Spots on Celluloid*, debuted in 1989, and his follow-ups, often compiled from Super 8 footage as well as video, highlighted the free-surfing action that surrounded the pro circuit as well as the renaissance of longboarding which he heralded with his 1994 effort *Full Circle*.

Bystrom shared other similarities with Bob Evans. He branched into publishing with a new magazine, *Pacific Longboarder*, which featured surfers from both sides of the Pacific, and also published books. His portfolio of new longboarding, *The Glide*, was published in 1998 but, tragically, Bystrom was killed in a car accident twelve months later.

The renaissance of longboarding and a renewed interest in the roots of the sport had baby-boomer surfers looking back to what most would consider their favourite surf movie, *The Endless Summer*, which had been Brown's last surf attempt at the genre, although he later produced *On Any Sunday*, a motorbike scramble documentary. The success of *The Endless Summer* allowed Brown to take early retirement, but the 1992 video release of his early surf features led him back into surf movies. He was then approached by New Line cinema who proposed he shoot a sequel. With over ten tonnes of equipment and a budget of 3.3 million dollars, Brown with his son Dana set out on another trip around the world, this time to shoot *The Endless Summer II*.

Brown retraced his steps around the surfing globe and with shortboarder Pat O'Connell and longboard surfer Robert 'Wingnut' Weaver, he followed the successful formula of *The Endless Summer I*, lacing the new film with corny humour, sunsets and quality surf action. Like ESI, Brown visited Australia, and like in the original, failed to find quality surf and was forced to labour through some corny travelogue sequences with Nat Young assuming the role of a surfing Crocodile Dundee. Although the film was beautifully shot and full of contemporary action and humour, it failed to have the same impact as the original and after a brief season in Australian cinemas ESII went to video.

While Jack McCoy was immersed in Billabong promotional videos throughout the 1990s, he also produced a video that traced the rise and fall of Billabong-sponsored surfer Mark Occhilupo. McCoy's 1998 feature *Occy – The Occumentary* covered Occhilupo's early career as a Cronulla grom and his rise through the rankings. By 1988, Occy's career had appeared to be over. He had withdrawn from competition and spent nearly a decade in a netherworld where he put on weight and spent long periods out of the water.

As far as surfing videos and movies go, *The Occumentary* was as close to a 'warts and all' expose as surfing gets but merely skimmed over Occy's retreat from pro surfing.

Occhilupo was back. He'd trimmed down and was enjoying surfing again with his hard-carving free-surfing style. Occy's rebirth was a breath of fresh air in a sport increasingly dominated by a generation of surfers who built reputations with their ability to tail slide and pop airs in sloppy beach-break mush.

⊕ Occie's comeback made headlines!

◉ Mark Occhilupo flies along a heavenly blue special at Snapper Rocks.

⊕ Wayne Dean looks like he's doing a bit of reef walking as he drops to the bottom of a Snapper Rocks wall.

Apart from a few skirmishes with the surfers 'wronged' by the ASA in the early 1970s, the surf media in general has always been reluctant to expose the 'behind-the-scenes' drug busts and dramas. But by the time the documentary hit the surf shop shelves, Occhilupo was back. He'd trimmed down and was enjoying surfing again, and Jack McCoy artfully captured some of Occy's hard-carving free-surfing style. Occy's rebirth was a breath of fresh air in a sport increasingly dominated by a generation of surfers who built reputations with their ability to tail slide and pop airs in sloppy beach-break mush. Occy can tail slide, but it's on edge rail carving that is his trademark. His forehand cutbacks are executed with the whole rail buried in the wave face causing rooster-tails of spray, but his back hand turns and long curl-skimming floaters are what have often brought him in the big bucks.

As he rejuvenated his career Occhilupo took out one of the world's richest pro events, the one-off Super Skins. The Skins event, sponsored by Rip Curl and retail chain Surf Dive 'n' Ski, followed the format used so successfully in golf tournaments. But instead of dropping putts for cash, competing surfers caught waves for cash, with

'I want to get back to the pure essence of surfing, that's my major goal. To experience that, is what I'd like to do in the future. I'd love to be sponsored again, travel, and make films. I'd like to portray myself in a "pure light". I think that my surfing is very valid.'
Shane Herring, 2000

Rabbit Bartholomew started his surfing career as a brash but stylish upstart from the Gold Coast who went on to take the World Title in 1978. Nowadays, he's less brash and more stylish – tubed at Duranbah.

each highest scoring wave gaining the surfer five thousand dollars and a place in the next round. The Super Skins event followed the 1997 Rip Curl Pro at Bells and in near-perfect, two-metre waves peeling through the Bells bowl Occy took out the event, picking up $55,000 and a new four-wheel drive in the process.

Occy's stunning comeback was a classic rags-to-riches story and the surfing press and general public showered him with more praise when in 1999, at the age of thirty-three, he took the world title, with young Aussie up-and-comer Taj Burrow runner-up.

If Occy's initial fall from grace could be attributed to personal problems, the collapse of the career of Dee Why surfer Shane Herring was partly attributed to equipment failure. In 1992, Shane Herring was sitting on top of the tour ratings, having knocked off Kelly Slater in the 1992 Coca-Cola Bottlers Classic at North Narrabeen. Like many surfers at the time, Herring made the switch to new refined Thrusters known as banana boards. These thin, narrow tri fins with exaggerated bottom rocker were great in bowly surf up to eight feet and could carve arcs on a two-cent piece, but without a sufficient planing section the boards often struggled to accelerate in sloppy conditions. Even so, nearly all the pros were riding them.

Banana boards looked like the next big breakthrough in surf design, so Herring went with them too. But the boards didn't suit Shane Herring's slicing style. His results suffered, and the high expectations of the media and his sponsors didn't help. He switched back to straighter bottomed boards but could not regain his momentum and within two years was out of the top sixteen, his competitive career over.

These thin, rockered Thrusters and the next evolutionary step in board design, the kick nose, were perfectly suited to pros, often surfing exotic and perfect waves with their quivers of finely tuned boards, but such craft weren't suited to the waves that confront the weekend surfers, frustrated by their lack of flotation and soft glass jobs.

It was this frustration with the tiny and easily dinged shortboard that was partly responsible for the re-emergence of long-board surfing and by the middle of the decade longboard blanks were being manu-factured in similar numbers to shortboard blanks. The new longboards featured the plan shapes and decorations of their primitive ancestors but were lighter, with precision bottom and rail curves, and although the retro single fin remains popular, Thruster versions have become just as common.

Their appeal is obvious: since they can be paddled with ridiculous ease, they are easier to catch waves on and are therefore easier to learn on. Which explains why so many girls are now paddling around in the line-up on longboards or mini-mals – sub-nine-foot boards.

The new longboards spawned their own competition circuit, with Surfing Australia conducting national titles and The Hog's Breath Café spon-soring the Australian leg of a world title tour. Initially the longboard revival was characterised by a complete infatuation with all things 60s, both in and out of the water. Nat Young, in his return to competitive surfing, dominated the fledgling longboard events, winning four of the first five world longboard titles, but back home he faced a series of talented longboarders, both young and old. One of them, Ray Gleave from the northern New South Wales ham-let of Cabarita, is a remarkable blend of polished casual styling, punctuated by long, long, long nose-rides and the most mannered drop-knee cutback this side of Phil Edwards. His nu-retro style forced Nat into the background and although an international title has so far eluded Gleave, he took out the 1991, 92, and 93 Aussie longboard titles.

Similar old-school surfer Wayne Dean, victor in 1999 and 2000, repeated his success of eighteen years before when he took out the national Senior Men's title on a shortboard! Deane is a seasoned performer who built a reputation as a skilled surfer in the waves of Hawaii as early as 1972.

Both Deane and Gleave have had to put up with a rampaging pack of progressive longboarders like Jason Blewett, Jared Morell, Gareth Donovan, Brett White and Beau (son of Nat) Young. Beau Young's progressive style, a blend of hard surfing, broken-arm style and contemporary moves, took him to the top of the longboard world when, in

⊕ Although he's a World Longboard Champ, Joel Tudor isn't locked in to any one style of surfing, he's equally at home on a thruster, or like here, heading back towards the curl on a short double ender.

Invest in Surfing's Past

Surfers who returned to longboarding learnt a few things about their old boards too: these ancient yellowing planks rescued from under the house have huge nostalgic value and can be worth big money. They have become surfing antiques, and a clean, unmolested signature model can now bring in a couple of thousand dollars. Even restored old dungers can be worth ten times their original price tag. Beautiful specimens can be seen in the 'old mal' section at most longboard events, where competitors lug the aged brutes down to the water's edge and relive the era before 1966. There's money to be made, and spent, on surf memorabilia, too: a complete cherry collection of *Surfing World* or *Surfer Magazine* makes a great superannuation investment. One avid surf collector does regular checks of the supermarket aisles, just to pick up a carton of Rinse Clean Surf washing powder. For the latest wave graphics, of course!

2000, he emulated his dad's 1966 result and without anywhere near so much hoopla won the world longboard title.

But when it comes to roots and retro there is only one surfer: Californian Joel Tudor. Tudor surfs and looks as though a glitch in surfing hyperspace has beamed him from 60s Malibu to the 90s, where he arrived as a fourteen-year-old longboard prodigy preaching the gospel of 'one god, one country, one fin!'

Had Tudor been around in 1965, he would have been one of the best ever, but there's more to Tudor than his Jetson's-like cool, and although his longboards replicate the Cali specials of 1965, right down to their straight rockers and heavyweight glass jobs, Tudor rides anything and carves. Anything from triple stringer semi-guns, rocket-fish and double-enders to contemporary thrusters. As the gleam of the new millennium brightens, look up 'all-round surfer' in the *New Dictionary of Surf*... you'll find a picture of Joel Tudor.

The big move of the 1960s – the long nose-ride – is also a defining move in 1990s longboarding, but like in the 60s it has become formulaic, with long nose trims out onto the safety of the shoulder; the surfer posing, one arm extended above the head and the other bent and folded behind the head. It's followed by a long cutback to the soup, followed by a bottom turn, the whole process then repeated. The infatuation with nose-riding and signature models that was discarded in 1966 is back, in all its one-dimensional glory.

Although the appeal of modern longboards, mini-mals and bodyboards attracted a new generation of women surfers, girls were still taking to the water on shortboards. Pam Burridge, Pauline Menczer, Jodie Cooper, Trudy

⤒⤒ Modern longboards can manoeuvre more tightly under the curl than their unwieldy predecessors. Josh Constable at Duranbah.

⤒ Huge slices of surfshop wall space are now devoted to girls' surfwear. It's not just bikinis, there's wetsuits, rash vests and accessories.

Todd, Lynette Mackenzie and Serena Brooke all shot to the top of the women's tour ratings on such boards, giving the latest generation role models and styles to emulate.

Until the mid-1990s, girls who wanted to hit the water usually had to make do with boardies, wetsuits and rashies scrounged from the 'XS' section of the men's racks in local surf shops. Surf-wear companies then saw an opportunity to cater for girls and added functional and fashionable surf wear to ranges that previously had been limited to bikinis, dresses, skirts and casual shorts. Quiksilver rejigged its ladies range, tagged it 'Roxy' and focused on young teen girls who wanted to be seen in the latest gear each

⊤ Serena Brook at the bottom of a clean fun-sized wall at Burleigh Heads.

summer, but the women's tour still had a long way to go to catch up to the men's events, certainly in terms of earnings.

In 1990 the prize money up for grabs on the women's tour was $257,000, which swelled to $364,000 by 2001. In a striking contrast, the men's tour events, worth $1,910,000 in 1990, had reached a cool $3,472,800 by 2001. Mark Richards took home $23,350 in his world title year of 1980. Twenty-one years later, the 2001 world title holder, Californian C. J. Hopgood, pocketed A$102,533 in contest earnings for his year on the tour. Not bad earnings for a young surfer, and what would you do with it? Well as Joel Parkinson put it in 2002, 'basically, I've got more toys and stuff, more toys to play with'.

'I was more into opening the **door** for the girl at the beach or at **school** who wants to go surfing.'
Pam Burridge, 1992

The main breaks of Kalbarri, The Bluff and Gnaraloo aren't the only quality waves on offer, but the other breaks are shrouded in secrecy and are subject to tight-lipped security.

⊖ Brendan Margieson snap frozen as he reaches the top of his arc on this left-hander in South Australia.

⊕ Thrusters have a small turning circle. Here's Sam Lamiroy measuring the shortest distance between two points.

In 1980 US women's surfer Margo Oberg won her second world title and earned $4750 for her year on the tour. By the year 2001, when Layne Beachley took the title, the available prize money had grown to $364,000. Layne Beachley, who has perhaps the best surfing surname going around, is the highest profile woman surfer in the country. Four-time world champ, Beachley's surfing is a mixture of style and typical Aussie aggression, a blend of slicing cutties and lip carves. She has won events in the grunt of the North Shore, the chill of Bells and the class of Kirra and in 2001 she won the Billabong Pro at one of the new world's most dangerous surf spots, Teahupoo in Tahiti.

Meanwhile, Kelly Slater's reign, which finally ended after the 1998 season when he retreated from the pro tour to spend more time free surfing, was a high point for US surfing. For years the Aussies had dominated the tour, but throughout the mid-1990s a committed bunch of Yanks filled the upper reaches of the ratings. Yet this was only a momentary glitch. A decade of intensive competition training, based partly on the Surfing Australia coaching schemes that endorsed coaches who passed through their intensive course structure, unveiled even more focused and hungry grommets.

'I think the competetive **surfers** of my generation left a rich legacy that has opened the doors of **opportunity** for following generations.'
Rabbit Bartholomew, 1998

As Occy was fighting his way back into championship contention he was joined by Shane Powell, Michael Campbell and two evergreens. From the Gold Coast came Michael 'Munga' Barry, who was raised in the barrels of Kirra and Burleigh; and, from further south, Novocastrian goofy Luke Egan. Egan's father Sam, a respected local surfer in the 1960s, went on to establish a successful board-building company. Jake Patterson, Taj Burrow, Nathan Webster and Joel Parkinson came hot on their heels. Parkinson's uncle, Darryl, had won the prestigious Duke Kahanamoku Trophy at the Aussie titles of 1975. The Duke trophy, awarded to the most promising surfer of the event, had increased his profile, but, like a lot of other accomplished 70s surfers, Darryl was happier surfing local Sunshine Coast beaches with his mates. Darryl had been tagged 'the next big thing' – a title that has haunted many surfers over the years. Joe Engel, Nicky Wood, Californian Joey Buran, and the Gold Coast's Jason Buttonshaw all failed to live up to that tag, at least in the competition arena.

The new millennium surf scribes are always looking to be the first to claim 'the next big thing' and the next 'next big thing' may well be Mick Fanning. He's from the southern end of the Gold Coast, and he and fellow locals Joel Parkinson and Dean Morrison are carrying on the tradition of MP, PT and Bugs – starting as young groms, honing their skills in the soft Gold Coast shore breaks, then graduating to the big time with their explosive surf skills. When they're not getting slotted at Kirra or Burleigh, these three 'Coolies' are out flying aerials in the Duranbah beach-break circus. Fanning is a special talent, a dynamic surfer who has sharpened his skills in the barrels of Kirra and the new Snapper sand bar. And although his loose, rubbery style is perfectly suited to snappy Australian beach breaks and point waves, he is equally at home in the bigger stuff and his 'tow-in' surfing in giant Gold Coast surf on the new bank outside Snapper Rocks has made a lot of people sit up and take notice. Some in the media say the world title is his for the taking, and surely a long professional career beckons.

'Perhaps the **aerial** is a little like the female **orgasm** – it doesn't matter if you don't make it, as long as you have **fun** trying.'
Australia's Surfing Life, 1995

Rip Curl, who started off as a rough and ready surfboard company, now market their wares all over the globe. As their business, and that of their rival's Quiksilver, has grown, so too has the once-tiny holiday town of Torquay. The road from Geelong to Torquay, once simply Torquay Road is now the Surfcoast Highway and the tiny coastal hamlet, with side streets that once led to tinier surf factories, has been transformed into a southern surf city.

Torquay is surf-city Australian style, with its Surf Coast plaza, an architectural mishmash of faux Caribbean and surf-deco – a plaza bursting with surf shops, corporate surf-dom office blocks and fast food stores. Torquay's saving grace is its surf – in particular, Bells Beach. The Torquay sprawl that climbs along the cliffs from Jan Juc stops just opposite the break of Boobs, where the Bells Beach Surfing Reserve starts.

In the years after the 1970 world titles, local surfers and ASA administrators could see the writing on the wall – sooner or later someone would sell up the rolling pastures behind Bells, and housing subdivisions would destroy Bells' rugged beauty. Victorian surfing administrators Tony Ollson, Rod Brooks and Stan Couper were instrumental in

⊡ Ever upward and outward – the Torquay sprawl.

⊕ Tommy Carroll, an elder statesman of Australian surfing, sends his stub-vector into orbit on the Sunshine Coast.

setting up the Bells Beach Advisory Committee, which was responsible for the reserve being proclaimed. After liaising with the Barrabool Shire Council, the strip of land behind Bells was set aside as a surfing reserve, and the land behind the reserve became a buffer zone, with restrictions placed on the size of any sub-divisions. Most of the restrictions are valid, and the fine print also states that dogs are prohibited in the reserve, as is the consumption of alcohol, and in what could only belong in the 'seemed like a good idea at the time' file, footy is prohibited in the reserve. (In Victoria this is sacrilege! It's like banning beach cricket!)

But thirty years after its inception, the reserve continues to protect the coastal environment from further development, and its Advisory Committee ensures that Bells is not swamped by endless weekends of surfing competition. A similar reserve is proposed for the Margaret River headland in Western Australia, but for the moment Bells is the only surfing reserve in the country and one of only two in the world.

Margaret River in Western Australia, at one time a haven for drop-out surfie types and now a thriving winegrowing region, is still isolated from suburbia, but isolation hasn't stopped surfers heading further along the continent's western edge and exploring the north-west coast. Up there is a shoreline of endless possibilities; and the main breaks of Kalbarri, The Bluff and Gnaraloo aren't the only quality waves on offer, but the other breaks are shrouded in secrecy and are subject to tight-lipped security.

Western Australia surfing identity Murray Smith recalls the early days 'up the coast' and describes some of the first sessions at Jakes at Kalbarri: 'They had Jakes to themselves all day, then picked crayfish off the reef in the afternoon and cooked them on the beach.'

Up this way, true locals are rare, and a few extra surfers in the water can sometimes lessen the odds of shark attack. But the coast is fragile and the exposed camping grounds can support only a handful of people at any one time. No one says you can't surf up this way; it's just that you'll have to find these waves yourself, by searching around and snooping along myriads of sandy tracks. Which is a lot more fun anyway.

On the other side of the country, Byron Bay and Noosa, both with their luscious surf and subtropical weather, have become special destinations for 'mexicans' (see definition) from Australia's colder climes and northern-hemisphere globe trotters. Both towns have fought off high-rise developers, and even though both are crammed with ritzy apartments and backpacker resorts, their charm, their beautiful beaches and their casual beach lifestyles remain intact. Both Noosa and Byron are sufficiently far from the suburbs of Brisbane that, although the urban sprawl has slowly claimed the Gold Coast, Noosa and Byron are safe. For the moment.

'I've got a friend who flies **spotter planes** for the tuna fishermen...and he's actually said he's seen three **twenty foot** white pointers **sunbaking** around the corner at Cactus.'
Phil 'Sharkbait' Horley, 1992

⊓ Western Australia's wilderness experience, and thousands of kilometres from a surf shop. Just don't ask where it is.

mexican n, someone from south of the New South Wales–Queensland border; a derogatory term commonly used by anyone who has lived north of the Tropic of Capricorn for more than two months.

Further south, just above the Victorian border, lies the Sapphire Coast town of Merimbula. For a time it was the preferred destination for Victorian surfers looking for warmer and longer waves. Admittedly, the water isn't a lot warmer, but the waves, when they're on, can be world class, and the waves at Merimbula Bar, a long looping left-hander at the mouth of the lake, in combination with the balmy climate, made this south-coast town a desirable option for surfers looking to invest in cheap coastal real estate.

Although Merimbula has grown, surfers have learnt the unfortunate truth about the surf. It's good, maybe even great, but it's inconsistent, and when the Bar isn't break-ing, the neighbouring surf spots aren't all that flash. But the bay between Merimbula and Pambula is great for sailboard riding.

In the early 1980s Phil Carrall, a local board builder, and Dare Jennings, a Sydney-based record importer and artist who had a holiday house nearby, started running sail-boarding contests. The contests were a big success, and their eye-catching posters and contest T-shirts had surfers sitting up and taking notice. Jennings started to spend more and more time on his artwork and T-shirt design and racked his brain for a brand ID that would be unique as well as hinting at the retro jazz and beatnik period of the early 1950s.

He combined his music and beat styling with the D-grade cult movies of the same era and came up with an evocative tag. He called his label 100% Mambo. Before long the 100% component of the label became superfluous, and with the assistance of a slew of handpicked weirdo artists like Mental as Anything's Reg Mombassa, Richard Allen, Rockin Jellybean and Jeff Raglus, Mambo became known for its T-shirts and out-there clothing, all plastered with colour and irony. They gleefully used their artwork to take pot-shots at the sacred cows of Aussie society, lambasting politicians, advertising campaigns, musical styles and, heaven forbid, other surf-wear labels!

Mambo was approached to design the uniform for Australian ath-letes to wear at the Sydney Olympic games of 2000. At first Jennings said no, fearing that the bureaucracy of the Australian Olympic Committee would stifle their attempts to create something uniquely Australian and Mambo-esque, but eventually they relented and, with Reg Mombassa contracted by SOCOG to recreate the biting satire of his art as part of the closing ceremony display, Mambo took its icons of Aussie suburbia to the world. Which wasn't what Mambo necessarily wanted. After all, it's hard to maintain that sense of irony when your T-shirts sell by the truckload and the commercial version of the shirt worn by Australian athletes is available in surf shops around the globe.

Merimbula, where Mambo had its genesis, is also famous for something else apart from its surf: sharks. Fortunately for surfers, as the fishing stocks have grown smaller, so too has the shark population.

Is there anything that scares Australian swimmers and surfers more than the thought of shark attack? You can be told more people drown, more people die from lightning strikes, that the odds are against it, but none of this makes any difference. If

'They had Jakes to themselves **all day,** then picked crayfish off the reef in the afternoon and **cooked** them on the beach.'
WA surfing identity Murray Smith

Mambo continues to poke fun at Aussie culture, while at the same time, and in a kooky way, it reveres it.

Surf habits of the blowfly

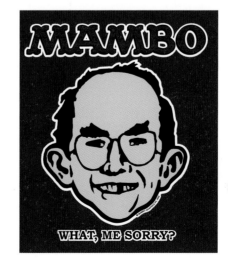

it's late in the arvo and you're swimming or surfing alone and you see it – a long shadow gliding, drifting, deep in the water beneath you, your heart leaps into your mouth, your eyes strain as they peer down into the watery gloom.

Is it a shark? Or, is it a stray branch of kelp, disguised as a shark, that's drifting along the bottom? Maybe you're swimming or paddling out, flopping down the back of a wave and there it is, a dark shape crossing the next wave of the set. A dolphin? A seal? Or the man in the grey suit? Odds are that it is seaweed, or a dolphin. Unless you're in the water in South Australia. It's the South Australian desert surf that has real shark problems. The breaks of Cactus and Caves and the coast around Port Lincoln are patrolled by Great White sharks – and surfers, professional divers and swimmers have all died from shark attacks in this area.

In the mid-1990s the racks in the new surf mega-stores were dominated by six-foot three-inch Thrusters, but now you can find an array of new-fashioned boards. There's longboards, all shiny and retro-striped, but there's also a new style of hybrid shortboard.

When Simon Anderson launched his new Thruster with wins at the Rip Curl Bells and Coke contests of 1980, he could not have foreseen what his breakthrough design would do. Once the Thruster took hold, it seemed that board design had reached an apogee, and apart from slight modifications like banana rocker, reverse vee and channelling, surfboard design stalled.

⬅ Taj Burrow floating, floating, floating.

Thrusters ushered in an era in which surfers were finally free to rip up and down the wave face, by breaking loose the outside fin; but the blessing of three fins is also their curse. Their toed-in, tipped out fins hate straight trim, they bog down horribly in sloppy surf or when a rider's lack of skill keeps all three fins locked in the wave face. Most recreational surfers have been forced to ride them because, until now, there hasn't been much else on the racks to choose from, and most shapers have been loathe to shape anything else.

Slop surf is often a good excuse to drag out your dad's aging board from under the house and try it out, and while old boards lack the explosive acceleration of Thrusters, they paddle easily and glide around sections with ease. Surfers soon began to make the connection and combine the flotation of a 1970s slug with the precision of contemporary Thruster fins and rails. Brian Witty's fin control system (FCS), which allows surfers to choose the best fin for the conditions and change fins with a minimum of fuss, has helped surfers experiment with the best of the old and the best of the new, resulting in the emergence of a small group of hybrid surfboards.

Wayne Lynch opened up hybrid possibilities with his Evolution boards – high-performance three-fin boards that suit surfers looking for flotation and performance. Small, blunt-nosed Snub-vectors, with various fin combos and new-generation twin fins

Rudders, Skegs and Fins The first skegs that took surfing from a wobbly glide to controlled angling were nothing more than small timber bumps on the tail of a hollow ply board. They quickly evolved to become fibreglass D-Fins, Cooper Fins, Dork Fins, Hatchets, Reverse Pixies, Tunnel Fins and beautiful timber laminates.

George Greenough took the skeg from an upright controlling rudder to a raked flexible fin that provided drive and power. Fibreglass and nails held early skegs in place but then basic fin boxes that enabled a rider to swap fins according to conditions appeared. The first fin boxes were nothing more than fibreglass slots, and Midget Farrelly added these to many of his mid-60s specials. By the end of that decade several boxes appeared. The WAVE Set box secured the fins with a moulded ratchet base that wedged them in. SAFE Set fins used metal screws to achieve the same effect. Although polypropylene boxes became more common in the early 1980s, the variety of fins available was limited and the fins often wobbled around unless jammed in with torn cigarette box lids.

A gradual standardising of Thruster fin sizes saw the introduction of the FCSs whereby each fin was screwed into a small fin plug. This allowed surfers to replace fins easily, and allowed the fin to pop out easily, which was great when travelling or when the fin connected with rocks, other boards or bodysurfers. Damage to the board was negligible, and a new fin was only as far away as the nearest surf shop.

168   **Blue Heaven**

Thrusters ushered in an era in which surfers were finally free to rip up and down the wave face, by breaking loose the outside fin; but the blessing of three fins is also their curse.

called Twinzers, cater for surfers who want some fun in small summer waves.

Geoff McCoy has taken the Lazer-Zap design that propelled Cheyne Horan to history at Bells in 1984, made it more user friendly and tagged it the 'McCoy Nugget'. The Nugget and a host of similar vehicles lack the aesthetics of Thrusters, they are round, blunt and stumpy, but they are fun. If you think of it in car terms, the Thruster has Lamborghini-like lines. And the Nugget? Well, think contemporary Mini-Minor! Advertising campaigns, surfboard showrooms and peer group pressure will keep intact the Thruster's reputation as the preferred vehicle of choice for most surfers. But bodyboards, longboards, mini-mals and hybrids are fast becoming the choice of surfers whose main concern is not their latest contest results. And if all you want to do is have more fun, more often, one of these vehicles might well be the answer.

⊕ The Gold Coast is the home of all that is tacky about Australian beach culture. Munga Barry sorts his way through the crass and commercial to snare this tube at Kirra Point.

I've got a theory — tube riding like this is easy ... you take off, aim for the boat anchored in the channel, grab the rail, close your eyes .... and pray. Shane Powell knows a better way.

From a Crystal **Cylinder** to a Crystal Ball

I was sitting in the back seat of a two-tone blue FC Holden Station Wagon as we zoomed back up the highway, heading for home after a weekend's surfing down the coast. The conversation with my mates covered numerous subjects ... like Neil Armstrong's recent walk on the moon ... and was it possible that blokes would actually grow their hair any longer than, say, an inch past their collar? Could mini-skirts get any shorter? And more importantly, at least as far as we were concerned, would surfboards get any shorter, or any wilder?

In the previous twelve months, I'd gone from a beaten up 9 foot 2 inch Barry Bennett to an 8'0" Wallace Widetail, then to a 7'10" George Rice Vee-bottom Pin, then to my 7'8" Klemmy Tracker which was roped to the Kennard board racks on top. We agreed, it wasn't just the length, these boards were 'far out' in comparison with what we had ridden the year before. Surely, by the late spring of 1968, no new board designs were possible.

We underestimated. Hair did get longer, mini-skirts did get shorter, and boards did get wilder. And we never could have guessed that the trusty station wagons and panel vans with their lo-tech reliability and valve radios would be replaced, firstly by the tappet-clattery, eight-track-equipped Kombi and then eventually by luxurious and funky four-wheel drives with sound systems capable of stunning local the wild life while plowing through bush tracks in search of a wilderness experience.

And it never occurred to us that an island off the coast of Antarctica –Tasmania — would offer not just a unique wilderness experience but perhaps Australia's largest wave. If you must have uncrowded surf, Tasmania may be the place for you. The west coast is still largely untouched and is blessed (or cursed) with an almost constant swell, gale-force onshores and very cold water. But the east coast of the island is another matter. At times a warm current meanders down from New South Wales, sending the water temperature up towards the 'comfortable' range and studding the shore with top-quality waves. Just out of Hobart lies a cluster of point breaks that rival (ignoring the cold)

the points of Noosa. Sure, these points need a big swell from just the right direction to break but there's five of them in a row, all lined with cobble stones, all long, all deserted, all cold, but the latest Tasmanian discovery, Shipstern, offers even more than isolation, and spectacular scenery…it offers grunt! It may lack the gigantism of Hawaiian mega breaks like Outside Log Cabins, Jaws on Maui, or Mavericks in Northern California, but its big wave siren call *has* lured Australian hellman Ross Clarke-Jones.

Clarke-Jones, from New South Wales' Central coast, had competed on the pro tour but with little success. He went on to make his name as a fearless big wave surfer, and when the development of 'tow-in' surfing allowed surfers to pick up monster waves, so big that they are impossible to catch by paddle power alone, both Clarke-Jones and Cheyne Horan made the switch and consolidated their reputations as premier big-wave surfers.

With tow-in surfing, the board rider, with feet strapped into a short, needle like mini-gun is towed behind a Wave Runner onto a green-cresting monster wave. As the rider is towed onto the green peak he is whipped across the face of the wave before it breaks and can set up his bottom turn well before the crest thunders over. But one mistake from the

⬆ Six clunky retro rockets on top of Carl Tanners Chev at Noosa. There's a lot of dollars in old fibre-glass and old chrome.

Surely, by the late spring of 1968, no new board designs were possible. We underestimated. Hair did get longer, mini-skirts did get shorter, and boards did get wilder.

➔ Mick Fanning scorches along the wall at Lennox Head.

Wave Runner pilot, or a snagged bottom turn from the surfer, leaves the rider trapped at the bottom of forty plus feet of whitewater. Wave Runners have big h.p. engines, which makes them extremely fast. But a forty foot plus wave is faster!

Despite the quality surf spots, Tasmania is yet to produce surfers capable of making their mark on the pro tour, which isn't to say that there are no quality surfers in the island state. Andy Campbell, Justin Hollick, Jy Johannesen and budding surf chick Dara Penfold are all following in the footsteps of 60s Tassie legends like Selwyn Stinky Burrows and Tony Hardie.

While surfboard shapes and lengths are once again moving into a period of experimentation, construction methods have changed little since the advent of foam and fibreglass.

Surfing became 'big business' everywhere else by the end of the 1960s, but generally wasn't seen as a promotional vehicle and only Coca Cola and Minties regularly used beach culture to advertise their products. That's another thing that back in 1968 we never dreamed would happen – that television ads that feature surfing would become a regular, if not nightly, occurrence in summer night-time viewing. But as to what may happen to surf culture next, well that's no clearer now than it was in 68.

Especially in regard to board designs.

The new millennium has seen a subtle shift to vehicles that have more appeal than the standard shortboard, usually because they paddle more easily. It seems that the optimum length for the shortboard has stabilised at around 6'3" to 6'5", and it's hard to see that changing – even though, after Rolf Aurness's win at the

⮕ Ray Gleave, Australia's longboard style master, takes a casual stroll to the tip. Just like the good old days!

↑ Taj Burrow plans his next move at Karates in Western Australia. First comes the cutback, then slap, bang, bottom turn, all the way to the shorebreak.

But although surfboard shapes and lengths are once again moving into a period of experimentation, construction methods have changed little since the advent of foam and fibreglass.

1970 world titles at Johanna, this was considered just a touch on the short side. Sub-six-foot boards have occasionally appeared, but anything this short is now considered to be a novelty length, or suitable only for a grommet's first stick, but surfboard lengths are once again moving into a period of experimentation, although construction methods have changed little since the advent of foam and fibreglass.

The thick woven Volan cloth that characterised the opaque rail laps of early longboards has been superseded by glasser-friendly Silene cloth, and new technology has improved blank-blowing techniques, but most surfboards are still made in small 'cottage industry' factories. No matter how intoxicating the aroma of resin may be, the chemical tang of acetone stinging your nostrils is a telling reminder that these chemicals are highly toxic, carcinogenic and highly inflammable. They are also non-biodegradable. The hundreds of thousands of boards that have been built since the early 1960s do not rot or decompose, and if they haven't become collectors items they're still out there, in garage rafters, under holiday homes or lying dormant in council rubbish tips.

Thankfully it *is* possible to make a board from environmentally friendly materials. Natural fibre composites derived from plants such as hemp and bamboo can be combined with blanks made from recycled styrene. These natural fibres, when impregnated with epoxy resins, create boards that are stronger and lighter than contemporary boards. Epoxy resin, although not entirely safe, is not in the same league as polyester when it comes to toxicity; and current technological breakthroughs may see resins made from sugar. So, with technology now available to produce a more environmentally sound product, why aren't these boards out in the market place? Quite simply, the industry isn't geared up for it.

To develop the new technology requires beefy capital investment and the cash just isn't available, and until a cashed-up surf entrepreneur decides to make it happen, or until some unknown ripper storms to the top of the ratings riding, say, a bamboo board, the consumer will have to choose: pay around six hundred smackers for a standard shortboard, or fork out around twelve hundred dollars for a bamboo shortboard (if you can find anyone making them – the most recent venture producing these boards is yet to make market inroads).

Surfboard wax production isn't much safer than surfboard production. Surfboard wax, originally a blend of beeswax and paraffin, is now made almost entirely from petrochemical by-products. There are thousands of surfboards out there, old and new, coated with who knows how many tubs of wax. Where does the wax go? Melted over the carpet in the back of your van? All over the inside of your boardcover or smeared over your wetsuit? Well, not all of it- try a walk along the shoreline at the end of a day when the waves have been crowded; you'll see the tiny flakes of wax washed up on the edge of the tide, where they stay.

The environmental issues that concerned surfers and the surf media in the late 1960s and early 70s have largely subsided but they

> **With technology now available to produce a more environmentally sound product, why aren't these boards out in the market place?**

Surfing Gets Organised?

The Australian Surfriders Association, which formed in 1963 to give surfers a voice on issues such as board registration and contest structure, is now known as Surfing Australia. The board registration issues of the 1960s died out long ago and the ASA went on to set up a structure of State, regional, national and international competition, as well as acting as a lobby group on issues such as beach erosion, environmental concerns, surfboard design and third-party insurance cover. Its role in surfing competition is unchanged, but over the years the scope and expertise of Surfing Australia has broadened. Although its roots lie in amateurism, Surfing Australia and its State-wide affiliates are responsible for the operation of all of the country's major pro events. Surfing Australia also conducts accreditation courses for surfing instructors and coaches, and, through a national network of Coca-Cola Surfing Australia Surfschools, delivers surf lessons and surf awareness programs to the general public. Since 1980 over two million students have participated. Surfing Australia's role in Australian surfing is wide but often misunderstood.

Perhaps it is seen to be mainly focused on contest surfing and less on local concerns such as water quality. In an ideal world, a combination of the expertise of Surfing Australia and the environmental conscience of the Surfrider Foundation could create a powerful lobby group which could protect the coast and beaches for the benefit of all Australians.

AUSTRALIAN SURFRIDERS' ASSOCIATION

The Box, an ugly, sucking reef break just up
the coast from Margaret River.

are still addressed by the Australian arm of the Surfrider Foundation. Its twenty-seven local branches concern themselves with monitoring water quality, litter, beach access and erosion, and they also arrange special events like the Ocean Care and Hold on to Your Butts days.

To date, the Surfrider Foundation has had small successes, helping to reach compromises on the Skennars Head sewerage outfall below Lennox Head on the far north coast of New South Wales, at Smiths Beach in Western Australia and at Sandon Point on the New South Wales south coast where residential subdivisions are planned. The organisation has sometimes been hampered by a scattergun approach to issues and although it receives government funding it still lacks financial support from most of our major surf companies. As their businesses grow and their coffers swell, these companies still need to address a concern that dogs all large industries – the amount of waste created. Cardboard cartons, plastic wrappings, foam shavings, blank and fibreglass offcuts all contribute to growing mountains of waste.

Let's jump forward from that surf trip of 1968, to around 1972, to a time of high-waisted jeans, airbrush shirts and crocheted bikinis, when a friend returned from California with a small rectangular piece of flexible foam, that she claimed you could surf on. Well, why anyone in 1972 would want to lay down on a half submerged wafer of foam and use it to try and catch waves was beyond my reckoning, but thirty years later, that wafer of foam — the bodyboard, has become the most popular surf craft in the water, and its eccentric creator is, well, pretty comfortable. And he's not the only one, some surfers

⊤ Layne Beachley slides along the lip. It's this kind of move that has made Layne our greatest woman surfer.

⊕ Noosa is crawling with these tanned young kids who flash you a big smile – as they drop in on you. They're not ripping you off, it's just that they love the vibe so much.

BISSO AT THE BOWER

Birdsall, Bisso, Wall, Cakebread, Raglus

John Severson, founder of the American Surfer magazine laid the foundations for surf cartoon art in the early pages of his magazine, firstly with his own graphic skills and later when he introduced a young Californian cartoonist, Rick Griffin, to his readers. Griffin created, 'Murphy', the first truly archetypal cartoon surfer, and the first Aussie surfing magazines quickly dropped surf cartoons into their back pages.

Australia's hottest goofy-footer of the time, Gary Birdsall was also a gifted artist and his work was common in *Surfabout* and *Surfing World* as was the art of Roy Bisson. 'Bisso' went on to illustrate with *Mad* magazine and *Penthouse*, while Birdsall continued his career as a graphic artist and still creates stunning images today.

Graham Wall's 'Eggie' was a regular feature in early editions of *Surfing World* then disappeared when groovier art took over in the mid-60s. Wall has returned, thirty years later to create 'Hang Ten O' Hooligan' in the pages of *Pacific Longboarder*. The legacy of these first surf cartoonists was continued, in the 70s by Victorian Paul Harris with his Griffinesque cartoons and posters, and in Sydney by Tony Edwards who took low-brow smut and gave it a more artistic bent when he created 'Captain Goodvibes' – Australian surfing's most famous mythic character.

Contemporary cartoon artist, Steve Cakebread continues in this irreverent vein with his adolescent creation, 'Felch', in Australia's *Surfing Life*, while Jeff Raglus after a career designing t-shirt prints and fabric prints with Mambo, is now a respected and offbeat artist. His successful kid's book *Schnorky, The Wave Puncher* is peppered with weird cartoon surf dudes based on the mates he surfed with at Point Lonsdale.

There's been a host of surf cartoonists down the years and maybe an archive of old school exercise books, if such a thing existed, would be most revealing, among them you might find dewy big-eyed horses, a proto rev heads' sketch of V8-powered, muscle cars, or scratched inside the back cover of some tousle-haired grom's homework a clumsy line drawing of a ribbed tubing peak with a cartoon surfer doing the unimaginable!

Don't let this happen to you!

'I'll have you know Sir, I'm no beach bum
– MY profession is tourist attraction!'

Clockwise from top left: Steve Cakebread;
Gary Birdsall; Paul Harris; Jeff Raglus;
Graham Wall; Gary Birdsall.

⊕ The new Snapper Rocks, Rainbow Bay, Greenmount sandbar in early 2002. By the time we went to press, it was still getting better.

have become rich, just from surfing; and others have built industrial empires and in doing so, have made themselves into paper millionaires on the stock market.

In surfing's first explosion, millionaires symbolised only one thing: 'the authorities'. Got that one wrong too.

But even Jimi Hendrix occasionally got it wrong. In 1968, he told us with that fuzz-laden voice, hidden deep in the psychedelia of his *Are You Experienced* album, that 'you'll never hear surf music aaagainnn'.

Surf music hasn't really come back, but there are still enough retro surf bands around to keep the spirit alive. Bands like Melbourne's Greasy Hawaiians and The Moment of Truth; Adelaide's GT Stringer; The Raouls from Sydney; and Mal and the Longboarders from Byron Bay. All plunder the roots of surf music for their salty grooves. The Cruel Sea, before Tex Perkins added his swampy vocal style, had their roots in reverb and delay, and the mighty Atlantics, who first set crowds stomping in 1963, are on the road again, touring the country with the 2002 'Long Way to the Top' national tour.

Thankfully, the sand mining program along Australia's east coast has ceased, and sand-starved beaches along the Gold Coast are being nourished by a new sand replenishment program. The last big cyclone season was in 1974 but, it's only a matter of time

before a big cyclone cruises out of the Coral Sea and, instead of dawdling over the tropics, makes a beeline for the Gold Coast. A repeat of the 1974 season would have disastrous results for beaches and property, so in 1993 local councillors, teams of overseas experts, engineers and a group of surfers led by Rabbit Bartholomew met to discuss the problem; their brief, to maintain a navigable entrance at the Tweed River mouth, to protect the beaches from wave attack and to maintain wave quality.

Just out of Hobart lies a cluster of point breaks that rival the points of Noosa ... there's five of them in a row, all lined with cobble stones, all long, all deserted, all cold.

The group came up with a plan to move sand around the Tweed entrance using pumps and bucket dredges, and by 2002 over 3.5 million cubic metres of the natural sand supply had been pumped or dredged across the Tweed. Although some of this sand is pumped onto the beaches, most is pumped to behind the wave zone and is gradually swept ashore.

By early 2002, the beaches at Rainbow Bay, Kirra, Coolangatta and Greenmount were the widest they had been since the 1950s. Unfortunately for beachgoers and their kids, the safe shallow lagoons in the corners of these beaches have filled with sand,

⊕ The Gold Coast isn't known for big surf, but every couple of years a low pressure system will sit out in the Tasman Sea and pump huge lines of swell up the coast. Brendan Margieson was towed into this blue monster, just off Point Danger.

Nathan Hedge at the base of a wave of
molten glass.

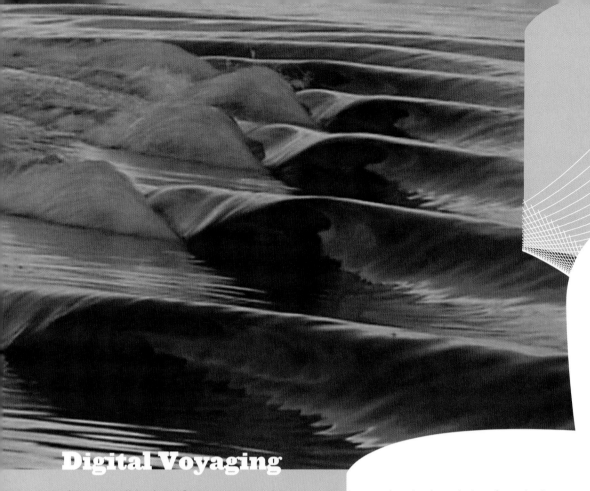

← Absolutely perfect lefts. For years the term 'perfect wave' was defined by the peeling three-footers that Bruce Brown, Robert August and Mike Hynson found at Cape St Francis. Monty Weber's mini waves are even better but can only be surfed in your mind.

Digital Voyaging

If you're still looking for inspiration about the care of the environment, look no further than George Greenough's latest project. Not satisfied with rejigging surfboard design, fin design or developing purpose-built cameras that allow him to shoot movies while surfing in the tube, George has decided to explore further the esoteric dimensions of surfing.

In his surfing short of 1973, *Echoes*, George tracked behind a dolphin as it glided just below the surface of a wave. Now, using a combination of film and digital enhancing, he has created a new film, *Dolphin Glide*. Using a rig attached to the bow of a runabout that supports a waterproof housing containing a state-of-the-art movie camera, George has spent endless hours following dolphins as they surf the waves of the northern New South Wales coast. His new footage, shot from within the wave as dolphins surf just below the surface, has been digitally corrected to enhance the shadowy light of inside the wave. In typical Greenough fashion, George hopes to release *Dolphin Glide* on DVD with an assortment of soundtracks … just choose your mood and set your stereo on stun! He also hopes to include *The Making of Dolphin Glide*, plus a book of stills from the film – and a virtual-reality dolphin ride! It's an ambitious project, fraught with financial no-brainers, but for George Greenough, it's the thrill of the ride, not the cost, that counts.

The digital technology that George is using is still in its infancy when applied to surfing, but imagine a miniature hi-res digital waterproof camera, mounted to the nose of, say, Mick Fanning's board while he takes on a four-minute ride on the new Snapper to Kirra sandbank, or Pipeline, or for real thrills, Teahupoo.

The technology is here, right now, and North Coast cinematographer Monty Webber's new feature, *Liquid Time*, released in late 2002, is a perfect example. Webber has taken a leaf out of the Greenough book of surf-movie production and come up with a stunning and esoteric piece that features no surf riding. Webber learnt his craft filming and editing for Paul Sargeant's *Surfing Scapbook* series of videos from the early 1990s and by then he'd already created his own experimental Super-8 surf movies.

In *Liquid Time*, Webber has captured perfect waves, and I mean Perfect waves with a capital P. But there's a twist: these waves are miniature, too small to surf, yet their perfect form and Webber's use of a miniature lipstick camera and super-slo digital technology have combined to create dream-like images that, like Greenough's in-the-tube shots, require mind-surfing. It's not the sort of feature that you sit down and watch after a few beers around the barbie; Liquid Time is too trippy for that.

forcing those beachgoers to paddle in a surf zone that now features a dangerous sweeping current.

But for surfers there is a huge bonus. The sand flow has swept along the coast, linking Snapper Rocks to Kirra with one long ruler-edged sandbar. When a stiff groundswell peels along this sandbar, waves sometimes peel for over a kilometre and surfers have been clocked spending over four minutes riding just one wave. Not only does the Gold Coast now have the country's longest right-hander, but the new wave is great, with long, high-performance walls and tubing sections. Some surfers claim that Kirra Point no longer has its quality tubes, but perhaps another good cyclone season will sort it out, realign the sandbank and return Kirra to its former glory.

But what if the big cyclones don't return for another decade? The sand will continue to fill up the beaches, and perhaps the world's longest right will just get longer, at the same time protecting the Gold Coast environment from cyclone-borne catastrophe.

The longest wave in the country hasn't made surf spots on the Gold Coast less crowded, and major surf spots in each state still suffer from huge crowds, which has led to some ugly incidents in the water and on the beach and Angourie had its fifteen minutes of tabloid fame, when Nat Young was hospitalised after a disagreement in the water which led to some unpleasant biffo on the beach.

Angourie was first discovered when Bob Evans's brother Dick stumbled across it in 1961 when he was looking for a spot to catch snapper. The Angourie he found that day was deserted; not a footprint in the sand.

For some, the joy of searching for a secluded cove caressed by lines of whitewater, has become a spiritual experience, for others the challenge of tackling the surf head-on is a highly disciplined athletic pursuit, but for most Australians going surfing, going down the beach, heading for the coast, whatever you chose to call it is, well, it's just what we love to do.

Dick carried his swim fins down to the waters edge and thought he'd give it a try, but the place looked decidedly sharky. He didn't fancy the creepy swim out to the take-off zone, so he walked to the end of the point, waited for a set, dove in, swam quickly to the take off and latched on to the first wave anyone had ridden at this spot, and cracked it all the way to the beach. He caught another six waves, making the trek out to the point after each. Then, when he'd had enough, he tried his luck with fishing, and caught a thirteen pound Snapper with his first cast. Dick Evans had found a blue heaven.

Being in the water, in the flashing, sparkling surf is fun, and fun for us all. For some, the joy of searching for a secluded cove caressed by lines of whitewater, has become a spiritual experience, for others the challenge of tackling the surf head-on is a highly disciplined athletic pursuit, but for most Australians going surfing, going down the beach, heading for the coast, whatever you chose to call it is, well, it's just what we love to do.

It's where we can sprawl in the sand on scorching summer mornings, or meander along the beach picking through driftwood on buffeting winter afternoons. It's where we can swim, surf, play beach cricket and pose. Its where we can check out the action, where we can party; the list goes on and on.

We believe in the beach, the waves and the surf.

They're our Blue Heaven.

⟳ The only thing that connects Mick Fanning to this Duranbah wave is his shadow.

Bibliography

Bede. Maxwell C. *Surf.* Angus and Robertson, Sydney, 1949.

Bystrom, Chris. *The Glide.* Chris Bystrom and Racheed Jameel Safady. Palm Beach, Queensland, 1998.

Champion, George and Sheila. *Bathing, Drowning and Lifesaving in Manly, Warringah and Pittwater to 1915.* Book House, Glebe, NSW, 2000.

Curby, Pauline. *Seven Miles from Sydney – A History of Manly.* Manly Council NSW, 2001.

The Duke Kahanamoku Corporation. *Duke Kahanamoku's World of Surfing.* Angus and Robertson, Sydney, 1968.

Guest, Thomas J. *Thirty Years of Hits.*

Published by M. J. Maloney, Craigieburn, Victoria, 1991.

McParland, Stephen J. *Beach Street and Strip.* Seagull Productions, Sydney, 1983.

— *It's Party Time.* PTB Productions, California, 1992.

Noll, Greg and Gabbard, Andrea. *Da Bull-Life over the Edge.* North Atlantic Books, Berkely, California, 1989.

Spencer, Chris. Nowara, Zbig and McHenry, Paul. *Who's Who of Australian Rock!* The Five Mile Press, Noble Park, Victoria, 1987.

Thoms, Albie. *Surfmovies.* Shore Thing Publishing, Noosa Heads, 2000

Warshaw, Matt. *Above the Roar.* Waterhouse, Santa Cruz, 1997.

Young, Nat. *The History of Surfing.* Palm Beach Press, Palm Beach, NSW, 1983.

Periodicals

Australia's Surfing Life – Morrison Media, Burleigh Heads, Queensland

Breakway – Breakway Productions, Seaford, Victoria

California Music – Stephen J. McParland. Concorde, NSW

Deep – Morrison Media Services, Newport Beach, NSW

Everybody's – Australian Consolidated Press, Sydney, NSW

SeaNotes – John Witzig and Co, Avalon Beach, NSW

Surfabout – Published by Surfabout, Cronulla, NSW

Surf International – Gareth Powell Associates, Sydney, NSW

Surfing World magazine – Breaker Publications, Manly, NSW

The Australian Surfers Journal – The Blue Group, Noosa Heads, Queensland

The Surfers Journal – Steve and Debbee Pezman, San Clemente, California

Tracks magazine – Emap Australia, Haymarket, NSW

Picture Credits

Endpapers: Shane Peel
Page ii-iii: Steve Ryan; Page vi-vii: Shane Peel; Page viii: Trevor Lemke; Page x-xi: Simon Williams; Page xii-xiii: Photos Phil Campbell/ boards courtesy Surfworld Museum, Torquay;

In the Beginning
Page 1: Albie Thoms' Archive; Page 3: Albie Thoms' Archive; Page 4, left: Albie Thoms' Archive; Page 4, right: Reproduced courtesy of Museum Victoria; Page 5: Albie Thoms' Archive; Page 6, top: Reproduced courtesy of National Archives Australia; Page 6, bottom: Reproduced courtesy of the Mitchell Library of New South Wales; Page 7: Albie Thoms' Archive; Page 8-9: Albie Thoms' Archive; Page 10: Albie Thoms' Archive; Page 11, clockwise from top left: Albie Thoms' Archive; James Northfield Heritage Art Trust; Albie Thoms' Archive; Gert Selheim *Australia for Sun and Sea*, 1931 © Nik Selheim/Courtesy Josef Lebovic Gallery; Page 12: National Library of Australia; Page 13, right: National Library of Australia; Page 13, left: La Trobe Picture Collection, State Library of Victoria; Page 15: Albie Thoms' Archive; Page 16, left: National Library of Australia; Page 16, right: Albie Thoms' Archive; Page 17, top: National Archives of Australia; Page 17, bottom: Courtesy *Geelong Advertiser* Archives; Page 19: Albie Thoms' Archive.

The Explosion
Page 21: Barrie Sutherland; Page 23: David Milnes; Page 24: Dick Hoole; Page 25: David Milnes; Page 26, left: *Surfing World* magazine, Author's Collection; Page 26, right: Courtesy Jack Eden, Author's Collection; Page 27: David Milnes; Page 28: *Everybody's*

magazine, Author's Collection; Page 29: National Archives of Australia; Page 30: Bruce Usher; Page 31: Trevor Lemke; Page 32: David Milnes; Page 34-35: Bob Weekes; Page 36: Barrie Sutherland; Page 37: David Milnes; Page 38: Mitchell Library of New South Wales; Page 40: Jeff Carter; Page 41: Bob Weekes; Page 42, clockwise from top left: Dick Hoole, Dick Hoole, Author's Collection; Author's Collection; Page 43: Barrie Sutherland; Page 44: David Milnes; Page 45: National Archives of Australia.

Surfing Goes Au Go-Go
Page 47: George Greenough; Page 49: John Quinn; Page 50: David Milnes; Page 51: Author's collection; Page 52-53: Barrie Sutherland; Page 54, top: *Surfing World* magazine, Author's Collection; Page 54, bottom: Dick Hoole; Page 55: Author's Collection; Page 56: Barrie Sutherland; Page 57: Barrie Sutherland; Page 58: Trevor Lemke; Page 59, left: Alby Falzon; Page 59, right: Author's Collection; Page 60-61: Barrie Sutherland; Page 62: John Witzig; Page 63: Courtesy John Witzig; Page 64: John Witzig; Page 65, top: John Witzig; Page 65; bottom: Dick Hoole/Courtesy Paul Witzig; Page 66: Bruce Usher; Page 67, left: Alby Falzon; Page 67, right: Courtesy Paul Witzig, Author's Collection; Page 68: Alby Falzon; Page 69: Courtesy *Geelong Advertiser* Archives; Page 70, left: Alby Falzon; Page 70, right: John Witzig; Page 71: Alby Falzon.

The New Counterculture
Page 73: Dick Hoole; Page 73/74, bottom: Rennie Ellis; Page 75: Dick Hoole; Page 76, left: Courtesy Midget Farrelly/*Surfing World* magazine; Page

76, right: Alby Falzon; Page 77: Courtesy John Witzig/Author's Collection; Page 79: Dick Hoole; Page 80-81: Dick Hoole; Page 82: Courtesy Alby Falzon/Author's Collection; Page 83: Courtesy *Surfing World* magazine; Page 84: George Greenough; Page 86: Rennie Ellis; Page 87: Martin Tullemans Visualz; Page 88: Dick Hoole; Page 89: Martin Tullemans Visualz, courtesy Gail Austen/Goodtime; Page 90: Dick Hoole; Page 91: Dick Hoole; Page 92: Courtesy Tony Edwards; Page 95: Dick Hoole; Page 96: Dick Hoole; Page 98-99: Dick Hoole; Page 100: Dick Hoole; Page 101: Dick Hoole; Page 102-103, clockwise from top left: Sheperd Usher Films; George Greenough; David Sumpter; Dick Hoole, Jack McCoy and David Lourie; Author's Collection; David Elfick and Alby Falzon; Posters: Author's Collection; Page 104: Rennie Ellis.

Surfing Enters the Mainstream
Page 107: Martin Tullemans Visualz; Page 109: Dick Hoole; Page 110: Martin Tullemans Visualz; Page 111: Surfinfo.com.au; Page 112, top: Joli; Page 112, bottom: Courtesy Dick Hoole, Jack McCoy and David Lourie; Page 113: Steve Ryan; Page 114: Dick Hoole; Page 115: Rennie Ellis; Page 116-117: Dick Hoole; Page 118: Author's Collection; Page 119: Martin Tullemans Visualz; Page 120-121: Steve Ryan; Page 122, top: Martin Tullemans Visualz; Page 122, bottom: Rennie Ellis; Page 124, top: Dick Hoole; Page 124, bottom: Dick Hoole; Page 125: Martin Tullemans Visualz; Page 126: Martin Tullemans Visualz; Page 127: Martin Tullemans Visualz; Page 129: Martin Tullemans Visualz; Page 130: Martin Tullemans Visualz; Page 131, top: Dick

Hoole; Page 131, bottom: Dick Hoole; Page 132-133: Joli; Page 134: Dick Hoole; Page 135: Dick Hoole; Page 136-137: Martin Tullemans Visualz; Page 137: Dick Hoole.

Surfing Goes to the Extreme
Page 139: Martin Tullemans Visualz; Page 141: Joli; Page 142: Steve Ryan; Page 143: Martin Tullemans Visualz; Page 144: Steve Ryan; Page 145, left: Steve Ryan; Page 145, right: Shane Peel; Page 146: Simon Williams; Page 148: Steve Ryan; Page 150-151: Martin Tullemans Visualz; Page 152: Martin Tullemans Visualz; Page 153: Simon Williams; Page 154: Simon Williams; Page 155: Simon Williams; Page 156, top: Simon Williams; Page 156, bottom: Joli; Page 157: Martin Tullemans Visualz; Page 158-159: Martin Tullemans Visualz; Page 160: Simon Williams; Page 161: Scott Wintle; Page 162: Joli; Page 163: Joli; Page 165: Courtesy of Mambo; Page 166-167: Martin Tullemans Visualz; Page 169: Shane Peel.

A Crystal Cylinder to a Crystal Ball
Page 171: Martin Tullemans Visualz; Page 173: Rennie Ellis; Page 174-175: Simon Williams; Page 176-177: Scott Wintle; Page 178: Simon Williams; Page 179: Author's Collection; Page 180: Steve Ryan; Page 181, top: Steve Ryan; Page 181, bottom: Simon Williams; Page 182: Roy Bisson; Page 183, clockwise from top left: Steve Cakebread; Gary Birdsall; Graham Wall; Jeff Raglus; Paul Harris; Gary Birdsall; Page 184: Martin Tullemans Visualz; Page 185: Simon Williams; Page 186: Steve Ryan; Page 187: Monty Webber; Page 189: Simon Williams.

Index